Teaching 21ST Century Skills

an ASCD
Action*TOOL*

Sue Z. Beers

ASCD

Alexandria, Virginia USA

ASCD®

1703 North Beauregard St. • Alexandria, VA 22311-1714 USA
Phone: 1-800-933-2723 or 1-703-578-9600 • Fax: 1-703-575-5400
Website: www.ascd.org • E-mail: member@ascd.org

Author guidelines: www.ascd.org/write

Gene R. Carter, *Executive Director*; Judy Zimny, *Chief Program Development Officer*; Gayle Owens, *Managing Director, Content Acquisitions and Development*; Scott Willis, *Content Development*; Gary Bloom, *Managing Director, Creative Services*; Mary Beth Nielsen, *Manager, Editorial Services*; Alicia Goodman, *Project Manager*; Georgia Park, *Senior Graphic Designer*; Mike Kalyan, *Manager, Production Services*; Keith Demmons, *Desktop Publishing Specialist*

Printed in the United States of America. Cover art © 2011 by ASCD. ASCD publications present a variety of viewpoints. The views expressed or implied in this book should not be interpreted as official positions of ASCD.

All web links in this book are correct as of the publication date below but may have become inactive or otherwise modified since that time. If you notice a deactivated or changed link, please e-mail books@ascd.org with the words "Link Update" in the subject line. In your message, please specify the web link, the book title, and the page number on which the link appears.

PAPERBACK ISBN: 978-1-4166-1327-5 ASCD Product #111021 n8/11

Quantity discounts for the paperback edition only: 10–49 copies, 10%; 50+ copies, 15%; for 1,000 or more copies, call 1-800-933-2723, ext. 5634, or 1-703-575-5634.

Library of Congress Cataloging-in-Publication Data
Beers, Sue.
  Teaching 21st century skills : an ASCD action tool / Sue Z. Beers.
     p. cm.
  Includes bibliographical references.
  ISBN 978-1-4166-1327-5 (pbk. : alk. paper) 1. Teaching. 2. Learning. I. Title.
  LB1025.3.B445 2011
  371.102--dc23
                        2011020549

18 17 16 15 14 13 12 11   1 2 3 4 5 6 7 8 9 10

Teaching 21st Century Skills

An ASCD Action Tool

Acknowledgments vii

Using This Action Tool...ix

RATIONALE

The Framework for 21st Century Learning 3

Designing Instruction for 21st Century Learning 8

Teaching 21st Century Skills..20

References..25

INSTRUCTIONAL PLANNING TOOLS

Creating a Well-Rounded Set of Learning Opportunities...................28

Planning Instructional Design 30

Sharing the Instructional Plan with Students 37

Additional Instructional Planning Tools..41

CLASSROOM TOOLS FOR STUDENTS

Selecting the Classroom Tools...46

Creating Your Own 21st Century Tools...199

About the Author 203

Related Resources...204

Downloads

Electronic versions of the tools are available
for download at **www.ascd.org/downloads**.

Enter this unique key code
to unlock the files:
GEC75-06D6D-2EE1F

If you have difficulty accessing the files,
e-mail webhelp@ascd.org or call 1-800-933-ASCD for assistance.

Acknowledgments

In 2027, my grandson Kadon will graduate from high school. It is difficult—if not impossible—to imagine what the world will hold for him at that time. He will have career opportunities in fields that don't yet exist. The knowledge and skills he will need to exist in his world cannot yet be defined. How will schools and classrooms keep pace with the changes needed to enable Kadon to be adequately prepared for his future?

There is no crystal ball that will provide an accurate picture of the future, but we do know that there are some fundamental skills and processes that we can provide students now that will lay a foundation for learning for their entire lives. That is my hope for this action tool: to ensure that Kadon, and my other future grandchildren, have the best chance for fulfilling and productive lives.

In working with teachers and administrators across the United States and beyond, I have witnessed the depth of knowledge and skill that they bring to their classrooms and schools. This action tool is dedicated to all of those education professionals who strive to ensure that students who leave their classrooms are fully prepared for the next phase of their lives.

The foundational skills presented in this action tool are based on the work of the Partnership for 21st Century Skills coalition, which has developed a vision for 21st century learning that will ensure that all students are prepared to succeed in a global community. The partnership's work helps define 21st century skills and how educators can carry them into any classroom.

Additional thanks go to all of those who have helped me form my own understanding of what it takes to create effective learning opportunities for students. Through my colleagues at ASCD, the writers who have shared their expertise in professional literature, and the

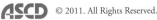

education professionals I work with every day, I have had the profound joy of becoming a better teacher, a better learner, and a better presenter.

The more I learn, the more I find that I still have much to learn. I hope this action tool can help those who use it to also continue to be lifelong learners and to improve their own skills and knowledge about teaching and learning.

The Partnership for 21st Century Skills has provided permission to use their model for this action tool. For more information on the partnership, visit their website at www.p21.org.

Using This Action Tool

This action tool defines the skills and knowledge that students will need for the 21st century and provides tools that you can use with any content to help teach and reinforce those skills. Based on the work of the Partnership for 21st Century Skills, the tools can help you design instruction that breaks down the walls between academic content areas and the application of knowledge so that students can be truly prepared for their lives in the 21st century.

Teaching 21st century skills is not about teaching a specific strategy or tool, but about teaching students a process or way of thinking about what they are learning. The goal is to help students think independently about the content and seek answers to their own questions. The tools and activities in this book can help you guide students through a variety of models and processes that allow them to practice making thinking routine. Through repetition and reflection, students can automate their thinking processes and routines and use them as they encounter new information.

Without students thoughtfully engaging and reflecting, the tools will not result in the kinds of habits of learning and understanding necessary for them to develop. Students must become fluent in their use of these new literacies and ways of thinking. The 21st Century Fluency Project (n.d.), a collaborative initiative sponsored by the infoSavvy Group, describes the type of fluency students should have:

> A young learner who is literate in the use of a tool, say a pencil for example, can use it to write, but does so haltingly because a great deal of focus is on the use of the tool. As time goes on, this learner will develop fluency with the use of the pen or pencil…. No longer will it be an impediment, instead their thoughts and ideas flow directly to the paper. The use of the tool is transparent. This is the level of proficiency we … strive to develop in today's learners.

The key to using the tools in this book effectively is to ensure that the tools

- Reinforce the desired way to think about and process content.
- Align with the desired outcomes for the learning.
- Are clearly presented to students, such as through modeling of how to use the tool.
- Provide opportunities for students to reflect on how the tools helped them process information and learn the content.
- Integrate technology appropriately.
- Allow for collaborative activities, where appropriate, to help students develop life and career skills.

ORGANIZATION OF THIS ACTION TOOL

To explain the foundation on which the tools in this volume were designed, the opening "Rationale" section describes the skills, or literacies, and knowledge that students need to succeed in the 21st century. It also illustrates the relationship among the elements of learning and how educators can integrate them into design learning opportunities.

The tools that follow are designed to help students learn and practice these 21st century skills. The chart on pages 46–49 identifies the 21st century skills to which each tool pertains. As you consider integrating content with these skills, the chart will help you identify appropriate tools for designing instruction and learning opportunities.

Each tool consists of

- A key that identifies to which 21st century skills the tool is linked.
- Directions that provide guidance for implementing the tool in the classroom.
- Tips such as how to introduce the activity, optimal grouping options, follow-up activities, and how the tool can fit into a larger lesson.
- Suggestions for integrating technology. Because the landscape and availability of technology is continuously shifting, the suggestions are generic. Some genres of technology that educators can consider integrating into learning opportunities include the following:

Purpose of Technology	Examples
Search for Information	Variety of search engines and browsers, such as Bing, Google, Yahoo, Ask.com, and Firefox. Also specialized search engines, such as Google Scholar.
Share Information	Social networking sites, such as Twitter and Facebook; e-mail; blogs; message boards; and collaborative editing tools, such as Google Docs.

Purpose of Technology	Examples
Create Multimedia	Microsoft Movie Maker, Creative Commons images, PowerPoint presentations, Wikimedia, Flickr, and Animoto.
Organize Information	Google Wonder Wheel, wikis, Diigo, PageFlakes, social bookmarking, and tags to categorize sites.
Collaborate and Share Information	Wikis, Google Docs, Diigo, message boards, social bookmarking, and Google Sidewiki.
Research Tools	Annotating websites, social bookmarking, Google Wonder Wheel and timelines, and Google Scholar.
Content Aggregators	RSS feeds and Google Reader.
Digital Conversations	VoiceThread, blogs, Twitter, Skype, webinars, videoconferencing, and PLURK.

(The section "Effective Use of Technology" on page 11 in the "Rationale" chapter goes into more detail about the infusion of information, media, and technology skills.)

• Questions that promote metacognition to help develop students' ability to think about their own learning and thinking processes. You can address the questions during class discussion, in small groups, in student journals, or in a variety of other ways.

To help create a well-rounded set of learning opportunities, start with the instructional planning tools on pages 27–43. With these tools, you can help students develop skills in all of the areas they need for success in the 21st century.

ELECTRONIC TOOLS AND RESOURCES

The tools are available for download. To access these documents, visit www.ascd.org/downloads and enter the key code found on page vi. All files are saved in Adobe Portable Document Format (PDF). The PDF is compatible with both personal computers (PCs) and Macintosh computers. The main menu will let you navigate through the various sections, and you can print individual tools or sections in their entirety. If you are having difficulties downloading or viewing the files, contact webhelp@ascd.org for assistance, or call 1-800-933-ASCD.

MINIMUM SYSTEM REQUIREMENTS

Program: The most current version of the Adobe Reader software is available for free download at www.adobe.com.

 xi

PC: Intel Pentium Processor; Microsoft Windows XP Professional or Home Edition (Service Pack 1 or 2), Windows 2000 (Service Pack 2), Windows XP Tablet PC Edition, Windows Server 2003, or Windows NT (Service Pack 6 or 6a); 128 MB of RAM (256 MB recommended); up to 90 MB of available hard-disk space; Internet Explorer 5.5 (or higher), Netscape 7.1 (or higher), Firefox 1.0, or Mozilla 1.7.

Macintosh: PowerPC G3, G4, or G5 processor, Mac OS X v.10.2.8–10.3; 128 MB of RAM (256 MB recommended); up to 110 MB of available hard-disk space; Safari 1.2.2 browser supported for MAC OS X 10.3 or higher.

GETTING STARTED

Select "Download files." Designate a location on your computer to save the file. Choose to open the PDF file with your existing version of Adobe Acrobat Reader, or install the newest version of Adobe Acrobat Reader from www.adobe.com. From the main menu, select a section by clicking on its title. To view a specific tool, open the Bookmarks tab in the left navigation pane and then click on the title of the tool.

PRINTING TOOLS

To print a single tool, select the tool by clicking on its title via the Bookmarks section and the printer icon, or select File then Print. In the Print Range section, select Current Page to print the page on the screen. To print several tools, enter the page range in the "Pages from" field. If you wish to print all of the tools in the section, select All in the Printer Range section and then click OK.

Rationale

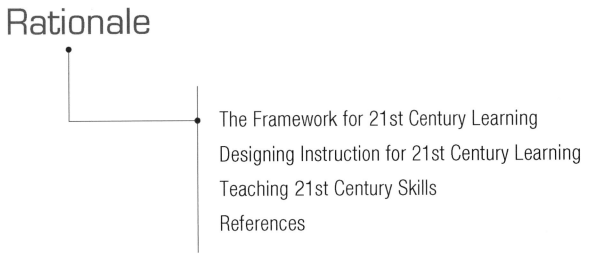

The Framework for 21st Century Learning

Designing Instruction for 21st Century Learning

Teaching 21st Century Skills

References

The Framework for 21st Century Learning

Already more than a decade into the 21st century, much has changed since midnight of 1999, when dire predictions were made about computers crashing as the new millennium approached. Since that time, technology has grown and advanced exponentially, giving us tools that bring the world to our fingertips and have made a truly global community.

As educators, what do we need to do to prepare students for this rapidly changing, technology-rich, interconnected global community? What does it mean to be literate in today's world? To efficiently and effectively survive and prosper in the information-laden future, learners will need the crucial skills of choosing, accessing, using, and applying knowledge to innovate, solve problems, and think critically about information.

A number of global initiatives have attempted to define the skills and competencies that students will need to succeed and thrive in the 21st century. One such initiative is the Partnership for 21st Century Skills, a public-private organization of major business and educational entities dedicated to defining a model of learning for this millennium. The partnership has defined a common structure and language that helps us make sense of the vast multitude of factors that we must consider in designing instruction for 21st century learning.

The Partnership for 21st Century Skills ([P21], 2003) identifies six key elements of 21st century learning:

1. It emphasizes core subjects at higher levels of understanding.
2. It emphasizes learning skills, such as information and technology skills, thinking and problem-solving skills, and interpersonal and self-directional skills.
3. It uses 21st century tools, such as digital technology and communication, so that students can "access, manage, integrate and evaluate information, construct new knowledge, and communicate with others" (p. 4) to develop learning skills.
4. Educators teach and students learn in a 21st century context that uses real-world applications and experiences that are meaningful and relevant to students.

5. Educators teach and students learn 21st century content in emerging areas such as global awareness and financial, economic, business, and civic literacy.

6. Teachers use 21st century assessments that measure 21st century skills in both standardized testing and classroom assessments.

The Partnership for 21st Century Skills describes the framework for 21st century learning as "the skills, knowledge and expertise students must master to succeed in work and life; it is a blend of content knowledge, specific skills, expertise and literacies" (P21, 2009, p. 1). The old literacies of reading, 'riting, and 'rithmetic—also known as the *three Rs*—are certainly still the foundation of learning and success in both school and life. However, a new set of literacies—also known as the *four Cs*—is moving to the forefront as students increasingly live in a global community with new technologies and expectations. The new literacies include

- creativity and innovation
- critical thinking and problem solving
- communication
- collaboration

Technology and social and personal responsibility are also important literacies for the 21st century. These new literacies are defined by the need for students to become thoughtful, intentional, and responsible learners and citizens, and they encompass the skills that students need to succeed in a rapidly changing world.

In short, the framework for 21st century learning is built on a base of academic subject knowledge that students apply appropriately through the essential skills of creativity and innovation, critical thinking and problem solving, and communication and collaboration. It is not a question of old versus new literacies; it's about carefully integrating the two to provide instructional opportunities that result in graduates who are college– and career-ready.

21ST CENTURY CONTENT KNOWLEDGE: EXPANDING ON THE THREE RS

The Partnership for 21st Century Skills' framework for 21st century learning is composed of core content knowledge, interdisciplinary themes, and skills that should be intertwined into a comprehensive set of learning opportunities. Students need to not only master the subject matter, but also learn how to use and communicate that knowledge.

All students should have a solid grounding in academic knowledge. In addition to the three Rs of subject-area knowledge, which are foremost in creating an academic foundation, students need a well-developed base of knowledge in areas such as

- world languages
- arts

- economics
- science
- geography
- history
- government and civics

However, students will lose interest and not retain knowledge if they don't learn content along with application and deep understanding. By applying the other two components of the framework, interdisciplinary themes and skills, students gain a deeper and more enduring understanding of the subject matter.

Interdisciplinary themes and skills allow students to recognize the interrelationship of ideas and make connections across academic subjects. When students create bridges of understanding among academic content, they move their understanding to higher levels and build lifelong habits and skills that cut across all content areas.

The Partnership for 21st Century Skills (2009) identifies the following interdisciplinary themes that span all content areas and that we should deliberately weave into the fabric of instruction:

- global awareness
- financial, economic, business, and entrepreneurial literacy
- civic literacy
- health literacy
- environmental literacy

In addition to these themes, teachers need to consider the connections among academic content when they design and deliver instruction.

21ST CENTURY SKILLS: THE FOUR CS

The 21st century requires us to create a generation of thinkers, learners who think creatively to solve problems and who collaborate with others at home and in the workplace. The ability to learn and create new ideas is essential for the 21st century.

"Workers must be equipped not simply with technical know-how but also with the ability to create, analyze and transform information and to interact effectively with others," (p. 3) remarked former Federal Reserve Board Chairman Alan Greenspan (2000) in encapsulating how we need to prepare students.

The 21st century skills that the Partnership for 21st Century Skills outlines—the four Cs—collectively address the kind of needs that Greenspan described, and teachers should

The Framework for 21st Century Learning

integrate these skills into every subject area. For these 21st century skills, students should be able to do the following:

1. CREATIVITY AND INNOVATION

Think Creatively
- Use a wide range of idea creation techniques (such as brainstorming)
- Create new and worthwhile ideas (both incremental and radical concepts)
- Elaborate, refine, analyze and evaluate their own ideas to improve and maximize creative efforts

Work Creatively with Others
- Develop, implement, and communicate new ideas to others effectively
- Be open and responsive to new and diverse perspectives; incorporate group input and feedback into the work
- Demonstrate originality and inventiveness in work and understand the real world limits to adopting new ideas
- View failure as an opportunity to learn; understand that creativity and innovation is a long-term, cyclical process of small successes and frequent mistakes

Implement Innovation
- Act on creative ideas to make a tangible and useful contribution to the field in which the innovation will occur

2. CRITICAL THINKING AND PROBLEM SOLVING

Reason Effectively
- Use various types of reasoning (inductive, deductive, etc.) that are appropriate to the situation

Use Systems Thinking
- Analyze how parts of a whole interact with each other to produce overall outcomes in complex systems

Make Judgments and Decisions
- Effectively analyze and evaluate evidence, arguments, claims and beliefs
- Analyze and evaluate major alternative points of view
- Synthesize and make connections between information and arguments
- Interpret information and draw conclusions based on the best analysis
- Reflect critically on learning experiences and processes

3. COMMUNICATION
- Articulate thoughts and ideas effectively using oral, written and nonverbal communication skills in a variety of forms and contexts
- Listen effectively to decipher meaning, including knowledge, values, attitudes and intentions.
- Use communication for a wide range of purposes (e.g. to inform, instruct, motivate and persuade)
- Utilize multiple media and technologies, and know how to judge their effectiveness *a priori* as well as assess their impact
- Communicate effectively in diverse environments (including multilingual)

> **4. COLLABORATION**
> - Demonstrate ability to work effectively and respectfully with diverse teams
> - Exercise flexibility and willingness to be helpful in making necessary compromises to accomplish a common goal
> - Assume shared responsibility for collaborative work, and value the individual contributions made by each team member
>
> *Source:* From *P21 Framework Definitions* (p. 3–4), by the Partnership for 21st Century Skills, 2009. Copyright 2009 by Partnership for 21st Century Skills. Reprinted with permission.

The four Cs are not new areas of focus for classrooms or even new goals for education. However, their importance in framing instruction and learning has increased dramatically. In a world in which information flows instantaneously to a global audience, never before have communication and collaboration been so vital. And creativity and critical thinking are paramount in a global economy that rewards innovation and in which routine tasks can be automated, but thinking cannot.

Designing Instruction for 21st Century Learning

To best create a generation of learners who are equipped to handle the world of their future, we must fuse reading, writing, and math with processing skills in all academic areas. The diagram below shows the relationship among the elements of learning and how educators can integrate them to design learning opportunities that result in 21st century learners and citizens.

Elements of 21st Century Instruction

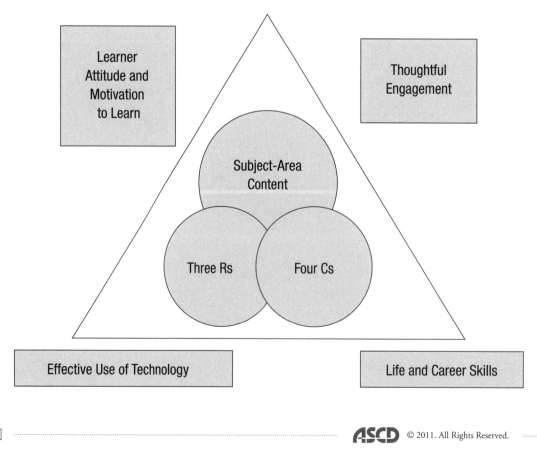

Designing Instruction for 21st Century Learning

The three elements inside the triangle illustrate the integration of subject-area content with the basic literacies of the three Rs and the four Cs, which provide students with the thinking processes and skills they need to use the content in meaningful ways. The blocks outside the triangle are other components that we need to consider in designing instruction for 21st century learning. These components include

- **Learner attitude and motivation to learn:** When planning instruction, we need to consider what we can do to create positive attitudes about the content and motivate students to take advantage of learning opportunities.
- **Thoughtful engagement:** Becoming critical thinkers and innovators requires students to be deeply engaged in the learning process and to reflect on the results of their learning efforts.
- **Effective use of technology:** Technology is a tool to promote understanding and manage information, and teachers should embed student understanding about and use of technology into lesson design. We should incorporate technology to help students learn effectively and efficiently.
- **Life and career skills:** We can help students develop personal and workplace skills by building in opportunities for collaboration. Instructional lessons can be designed to provide students with opportunities to take responsibility for their work, be accountable for the outcomes, and reflect on how well they have used life and career skills to complete the learning task.

The following sections explore each of these learning components in more detail.

LEARNER ATTITUDE AND MOTIVATION TO LEARN

Students who are used to being passive learners who accept the conclusions and constructs that are handed to them may not so readily accept the hard work of becoming true thinkers who actively construct knowledge. Thinking, creating, and problem solving are messy processes. Students must learn how to take new information and create valid schemas of understanding that make sense to themselves and others.

To engage students in this messy process of thinking, we must first make the process explicit by modeling. Because thinking is an invisible process, we need to provide direct, explicit instruction on the processes that help us create, think critically, solve problems, and communicate our understanding and that we want students to emulate.

The goal is to help students learn how to think, inquire, question, and solve problems and use these skills in new situations with new information. To guide students in developing these skills, teachers should

1. Make thinking visible by teaching students the steps in the cognitive process.
2. Model the process using familiar content and by sharing their own thinking as they model it.
3. Help students identify crucial steps in the process or those that are most difficult for them. Ask students to reflect on how to effectively manage these steps.
4. Give students a graphic organizer or visual map of the process to increase their understanding and provide guidance through the steps.
5. After modeling with the whole class, provide guided practice with feedback as students practice the skill in groups or alone.
6. Continually provide opportunities for reflection and discussion about the thinking students use as they work through the cognitive process.
7. Ask students to consider how they could use these thinking processes in new situations.

Meaningful thinking also requires students to assign personal understanding to concepts and processes so that they can see how the information or skill can be helpful in their own lives or futures. This personalization of learning sparks interest and motivation. In the "multitasking, multifaceted, technology-driven, diverse, vibrant world" (P21, 2003, p. 4) that students live in, images and knowledge come from a multitude of sources. Students learn what they pay attention to, and they pay attention to what interests them.

We must design instruction that grabs their attention, inspires them to learn, and convinces them of the relevance of that learning. Creating intellectual challenges that are neither too difficult nor too easy helps build students' interest in the topic. Then giving students the tools and strategies, or thinking skills, they need to be successful in their quest for understanding gives them the confidence and inspiration to accept the challenge. Learning is ultimately in the hands of the students.

THOUGHTFUL ENGAGEMENT

Metacognition is an engagement in a mental dialogue about our thinking. It consists of reflecting on how we process information, use that information, and behave as a result of our thinking. To hone their learning and innovation skills, students need to get into the habit of questioning their thinking, reflecting on how they use information, and reflecting on the thinking processes that they employed. Through this reflection, students become more cognizant of their "ways of knowing" and can learn how to strengthen their thought processes as they solve problems, think critically, innovate and create, and communicate and work with others.

Teachers can help students become more metacognitive by sharing their own mental models, reflections, and thinking habits. Teachers can also create strong learning opportunities for students that include a metacognitive component, which asks students to examine their own thinking and reflect on *how* they think, not just *what* they think. Metacognitive activities include components of reflection and sharing with others, and they should directly relate to both the content and the development of thinking routines.

The goal is to help students become independent thinkers who seek new ideas and solutions that go beyond the ordinary, and who communicate those ideas in collaboration with others.

EFFECTIVE USE OF TECHNOLOGY

Students today are bombarded with a wide range of technology tools and media that are constantly changing. Rapid changes in technology require students to gain new skills in accessing, managing, and using information.

New technology has made knowing information much less valuable than knowing how to find and use that information in new and meaningful ways. Helping students sort through the avalanche of information available—literally at their fingertips—and extracting the information they need for a task or situation is a critical skill in the 21st century.

To access and use information appropriately, students must develop

- **Information literacy** to use appropriate strategies for accessing, evaluating, and using or managing information.
- **Media literacy** to understand the messages being conveyed, how those messages are constructed, and for what purpose.
- **Information, communications, and technology (ICT) literacy** to choose and use appropriate technology tools. (P21, 2009)

INFORMATION LITERACY

Access and Evaluate Information
- Access information efficiently (time) and effectively (sources)
- Evaluate information critically and competently

> **Use and Manage Information**
> - Use information accurately and creatively for the issue or problem at hand
> - Manage the flow of information from a wide variety of sources
> - Apply a fundamental understanding of the ethical/legal issues surrounding the access and use of information
>
> *Source:* From *P21 Framework Definitions* (p. 5), by the Partnership for 21st Century Skills, 2009. Copyright 2009 by Partnership for 21st Century Skills. Reprinted with permission.

Accessing information today is not a problem; finding the *right* information in an efficient and effective way is the key. Students must have a plan for getting and using the information and ask themselves questions such as

- What information do I need?
- For what purpose will I use the information?
- What are the best sources for the information?
- What is my search strategy?
- How do I judge the credibility of the information?
- How can I organize the information in meaningful ways?
- Which technology tools are most appropriate for sharing the information?

Students must then use that information in legal and ethical ways. The concept of plagiarism was difficult enough for students to grasp when they were processing printed text only. Now with online sources of information from all forms of media, students must understand and comply with the legalities and ethics of using information from these diverse sources.

MEDIA LITERACY

> **Analyze Media**
> - Understand how and why media messages are constructed, and for what purposes
> - Examine how individuals interpret messages differently, how values and points of view are included or excluded, and how media can influence beliefs and behaviors
> - Apply a fundamental understanding of the ethical/legal issues surrounding the access and use of media
>
> **Create Media Products**
> - Understand and utilize the most appropriate media creation tools, characteristics and conventions
> - Understand and effectively utilize the most appropriate expressions and interpretations in diverse, multicultural environments
>
> *Source:* From *P21 Framework Definitions* (p. 5), by the Partnership for 21st Century Skills, 2009. Copyright 2009 by Partnership for 21st Century Skills. Reprinted with permission.

Designing Instruction for 21st Century Learning

Studying media begins with understanding the messages it conveys, and being aware of how media affects your thinking and action is a large part of becoming media literate. Beyond being able to analyze and interpret media messages, students must learn how to create effective communications using media tools. Understanding how different perspectives can result in different interpretations of the message is a crucial skill in effectively using and communicating with various forms of media.

INFORMATION, COMMUNICATIONS, AND TECHNOLOGY LITERACY

> **Apply Technology Effectively**
> - Use technology as a tool to research, organize, evaluate and communicate information
> - Use digital technologies (computers, PDAs, media players, GPS, etc.), communication/networking tools and social networks appropriately to access, manage, integrate, evaluate and create information to successfully function in a knowledge economy
> - Apply a fundamental understanding of the ethical/legal issues surrounding the access and use of information technologies
>
> *Source:* From *P21 Framework Definitions* (pp. 5–6), by the Partnership for 21st Century Skills, 2009. Copyright 2009 by Partnership for 21st Century Skills. Reprinted with permission.

In the digital world, new applications and programs are constantly being developed and others disappear. Rather than focusing on learning a particular program or tool, students need to be aware of the genres of technology that are available and how they can use these tools to become better thinkers and communicators.

Digital literacy, according to both national and international frameworks, consists of students being able to

- **Access:** Know how to search for, find, and retrieve information digitally (e.g., conduct an Internet search using a variety of search engines and browsers).
- **Manage:** Put accessed information into an organized structure for future access or application of the information (e.g., create a wiki, use RSS feeds, social bookmarking).
- **Integrate:** Use technology tools to synthesize, summarize, compare, and classify information from multiple sources (e.g., create charts, tables, spreadsheets, content aggregators).
- **Evaluate:** Judge the usefulness of information for a given purpose as well as its quality, relevance, validity, and appropriateness (e.g., use criteria to evaluate the source and content).
- **Create:** Use information to create new ideas by adapting it or applying it; putting information to use in a way that does not already exist (e.g., write a recommendation, film a video, create tables).

- **Communicate:** Use an appropriate technology to share information with an audience (e.g., use Facebook, Twitter, blogs).
(Kempster Group, 2008)

Regardless of the specific digital tool or application we employ in our instruction, it is important to help students learn the underlying skills for using information and communication technology efficiently and effectively. These underlying skills, the *five As of inquiry*, help students learn how to

- **Ask:** Plan an effective inquiry by asking the right questions.
- **Answer:** Gather the necessary information to adequately answer the questions and assess the validity of the information.
- **Analyze:** Make sense of the information by synthesizing and analyzing it.
- **Apply:** Use the learning in a context that demonstrates new learning and understandings related to the original inquiry.
- **Assess:** Reflect on the learning by assessing the use of the technology, the process of conducting the inquiry, and the thinking processes employed in the learning.

LIFE AND CAREER SKILLS

A study of employers' perspectives on the readiness of entrants into the workforce found that students need both academic skills and the ability to apply those skills (Casner-Lotto & Barrington, 2006). In ratings of what is "very important," the top four skills employers identified in the study (Casner-Lotto & Barrington, 2006) were application skills:

1. professionalism and work ethic
2. oral and written communication
3. teamwork and collaboration
4. critical thinking and problem solving

The fifth "very important" skill was reading comprehension. In addition, numerous reports have indicated that creativity and innovation are the most important factors in keeping national competitiveness in a global environment (Casner-Lotto & Barrington, 2006).

Content is the foundation for learning, but it is how students use this knowledge foundation that will make the difference in their ability to succeed in the workplace. In applying these skills, students need to use new knowledge in new ways to be able to adapt to a changing world. For the world of work, students need to be able to apply their content knowledge with 21st century skills in the following ways:

- **Critical thinking and problem solving**—Employ sound reasoning; think analytically; and use knowledge, facts, and data to solve problems.

Designing Instruction for 21st Century Learning

- **Creativity and innovation**—Demonstrate originality and inventiveness in work, communicate new ideas to others, and integrate knowledge across different content areas.
- **Communication**—Articulate thoughts and ideas clearly and effectively, including through public speaking. Write clearly and effectively to convey ideas.
- **Collaboration**—Build collaborative relationships with colleagues and customers, be able to work with diverse teams, and be able to negotiate and manage conflicts. Learn from and work with individuals representing diverse cultures, races, ages, genders, religions, lifestyles, and viewpoints.
- **Information, media, and ICT literacy**—Select and use appropriate technology to accomplish a given task and use technology to solve problems.
- **Life and career skills**—Leverage the strengths of others to achieve common goals and use interpersonal skills to coach and develop others. Continuously acquire new knowledge and skills, monitor one's own learning needs, and learn from one's mistakes. Take personal accountability and demonstrate effective work habits (e.g., punctuality, working productively with others, managing time and workload). Demonstrate integrity and ethical behavior, and act responsibly with the interests of the larger community in mind.

Beyond content knowledge and application skills, students must develop personal skills related to self-regulation and working with others to be productive and efficient workers and citizens. These personal skills include

- flexibility and adaptability
- initiative and self-direction
- social and cross-cultural skills
- productivity and accountability
- leadership and responsibility

Although these life and career skills are not easy to teach or assess, we can nurture them by providing students with good examples in action and giving them tools for understanding and reflecting on the skills. Each of the personal skills is described in more depth below. You can use the reflection questions for each to help students improve and think about how well they use these skills.

FLEXIBILITY AND ADAPTABILITY

Adapt to Change
- Adapt to varied roles, job responsibilities, schedules and contexts
- Work effectively in a climate of ambiguity and changing priorities

  15

Designing Instruction for 21st Century Learning

> **Be Flexible**
> - Incorporate feedback effectively
> - Deal positively with praise, setbacks and criticism
> - Understand, negotiate and balance diverse views and beliefs to reach workable solutions, particularly in multicultural environments
>
> *Source:* From *P21 Framework Definitions* (p. 6), by the Partnership for 21st Century Skills, 2009. Copyright 2009 by Partnership for 21st Century Skills. Reprinted with permission.

Reflection Questions for Students

- What changes have you encountered in your life? Give an example of a positive and a negative change.
- How do you react to change that is not of your own choice?
- How willing are you to change your opinion when new information warrants it?
- Are you open to feedback from others?
- How do you handle negative feedback?
- How do you handle positive feedback?
- Do you use honest feedback from others to change in positive ways?
- How do you evaluate information to determine whether it justifies a change in thinking or action?
- Do you keep an open mind to others' ideas? Give an example of a situation in which you felt you were open-minded.
- Do you search for new information when making a decision?
- What do you do when you encounter information that conflicts with your own knowledge?

INITIATIVE AND SELF-DIRECTION

> **Manage Goals and Time**
> - Set goals with tangible and intangible success criteria
> - Balance tactical (short-term) and strategic (long-term) goals
> - Use time and manage workload efficiently
>
> **Work Independently**
> - Monitor, define, prioritize and complete tasks without direct oversight

Designing Instruction for 21st Century Learning

Be Self-Directed Learners
- Go beyond basic mastery of skills and/or curriculum to explore and expand one's own learning and opportunities to gain expertise
- Demonstrate initiative to advance skill levels toward a professional level
- Demonstrate commitment to learning as a lifelong process
- Reflect critically on past experiences in order to inform future progress

Source: From *P21 Framework Definitions* (p. 6), by the Partnership for 21st Century Skills, 2009. Copyright 2009 by Partnership for 21st Century Skills. Reprinted with permission.

Reflection Questions for Students

- When have you taken initiative to direct your own learning?
- How do you manage time? What could you do to improve your time-management skills?
- What causes you to get off track in completing a project or task? What can you do to stay focused?
- What personal goals do you have for learning?
- What criteria can or do you use for prioritizing tasks?
- How will managing your time more effectively help you become a better learner?
- How will taking initiative be important in your future career? How is it important in school?

SOCIAL AND CROSS-CULTURAL SKILLS

Interact Effectively with Others
- Know when it is appropriate to listen and when to speak
- Conduct yourself in a respectable, professional manner

Work Effectively in Diverse Teams
- Respect cultural differences and work effectively with people from a range of social and cultural backgrounds
- Respond open-mindedly to different ideas and values
- Leverage social and cultural differences to create new ideas and increase both innovation and quality of work

Source: From *P21 Framework Definitions* (pp. 6–7), by the Partnership for 21st Century Skills, 2009. Copyright 2009 by Partnership for 21st Century Skills. Reprinted with permission.

Designing Instruction for 21st Century Learning

Reflection Questions for Students

- What social skills do you think are important in working with others?
- How could you most appropriately deal with someone who expresses an opinion that differs from yours?
- In what ways do you promote getting along with others?
- How can using social skills result in a better interaction with others?
- How can you acknowledge someone's different perspective while maintaining your own?
- Do you listen effectively to others without prejudging them or their ideas? Why might it be important to do so?
- How might understanding another person's culture or background help you understand their point of view?
- Why is it important to be able to communicate effectively with others of different social or cultural backgrounds?

PRODUCTIVITY AND ACCOUNTABILITY

Manage Projects
- Set and meet goals, even in the face of obstacles and competing pressures
- Prioritize, plan and manage work to achieve the intended result

Produce Results
- Demonstrate attributes associated with producing high-quality products including the abilities to:
    - Work positively and ethically
    - Manage time and projects effectively
    - Multitask
    - Participate actively, as well as be reliable and punctual
    - Present oneself professionally and with proper etiquette
    - Collaborate and cooperate effectively with teams
    - Respect and appreciate team diversity
    - Be accountable for results

Source: From *Framework Definitions* (p. 7), by the Partnership for 21st Century Skills, 2009. Copyright 2009 by Partnership for 21st Century Skills. Reprinted with permission.

Reflection Questions for Students

- Do you take responsibility for your actions? Why or why not? Give an example of an instance in which you took responsibility for your actions.
- Why is it important to set clear goals when undertaking a project?
- How do you manage time when completing a project?
- How could you better manage your time?

Designing Instruction for 21st Century Learning

- What criteria describe professional behavior?
- Think of a situation in which another person did not take responsibility for his or her actions. How did this affect others who were involved?
- If you were an employer, what work habits would you want your employees to have?
- What is your greatest strength in terms of being productive or accountable? What area is in greatest need of improvement?

LEADERSHIP AND RESPONSIBILITY

Guide and Lead Others
- Use interpersonal and problem-solving skills to influence and guide others toward a goal
- Leverage the strengths of others to accomplish a common goal
- Inspire others to reach their very best via example and selflessness
- Demonstrate integrity and ethical behavior in using influence and power

Be Responsible to Others
- Act responsibly with the interests of the larger community in mind

Source: From *P21 Framework Definitions* (p. 7), by the Partnership for 21st Century Skills, 2009. Copyright 2009 by Partnership for 21st Century Skills. Reprinted with permission.

Reflection Questions for Students

- What are the qualities of a good leader?
- Would you make a good leader? Why or why not?
- What could you do to improve your leadership style and skills?
- Give some examples of good leadership in action.
- How is being a good follower as important as being a good leader?
- What qualities of a leader are most important to you?
- Give an example of a time when you were in a position of leadership. What was positive about the experience? What were the negatives?
- What kind of leadership style most attracts you? What kind of leader are you most apt to follow?

Teaching 21st Century Skills

The workplace and jobs have changed drastically over the last 100 years, but today's schools look much the same as they did in the last century. The knowledge and skills taught in contemporary classrooms are many times misaligned with the knowledge and skills that students need to be prepared for their future and not our past. Our connected, global world calls for different learning opportunities and newly designed curriculum, instruction, and assessment.

New technologies, global competition and communication, social networking, and the accelerated growth of knowledge are changing the way we learn, live, and work. And in this global community, students have unprecedented access to knowledge and information. Schools and classrooms need to help students use this access appropriately, confidently, and with purpose.

Our challenge is to help students develop these skills while continuing to give them a strong foundation of knowledge that allows them full access to and participation in a world that is constantly evolving. Education that prepares students for the future is all about creating learning opportunities in which learners create their own knowledge.

We are moving from an education model of students and teachers to one of learners and facilitators. Although there are fundamental skills and knowledge that form the foundation of every subject area, the concept of a finite, concrete knowledge base is increasingly difficult to define. Classrooms need to become learning studios in which students design their own pathways to knowledge and understanding. In essence, we will teach less but students will learn more.

The more students know about a topic, the greater the possibility that they can create new ideas and solve problems—but just knowing isn't enough. We must design schools and classrooms that bridge the profound gap between what students learn in school and the knowledge, skills, and predispositions they need in 21st century communities and workplaces.

Instruction geared toward preparing students for the future will require us to cultivate students' cognitive skills by developing learning opportunities that focus on comparing, analyzing, elaborating, and organizing important concepts in academic fields. If they don't learn facts while concurrently thinking about how to interpret and use those facts, students won't retain the information.

TEACHING CREATIVITY AND INNOVATION

To create, students must possess a deep understanding of both the content and creative processes that generate innovations. Students cannot create from nothing, and "the deeper knowledge a learner has, the more analytical, experimental, and creative are that learner's thought processes (Willingham, 2007)" (Costa, 2008, p. 22).

Being creative requires a safe learning environment in which ideas are accepted, mistakes are acknowledged, and students are free from harassment. This environment provides students with an intellectual comfort and safety zone where they can feel free to experiment and try new ideas.

Classrooms that inspire creativity also inspire a sense of wonder as students ponder alternative scenarios, such as "I wonder what would happen if…" or "Suppose you did it this way." This creative use of knowledge and information is followed by critical thinking about generated solutions, including explanations, rationale, and details or examples.

In helping students learn to become creative thinkers and innovators, it is important that students

- Have enough knowledge about the content or subject to generate ideas.
- Clearly understand the need, problem, or situation that the innovation will fill.
- Examine the situation or problem from multiple perspectives.
- Conduct additional research or gather additional information as needed to establish a solid foundation of understanding.
- Create solutions or ideas based on the identified needs.
- Explain their ideas or solutions to others.

TEACHING CRITICAL THINKING AND PROBLEM SOLVING

The ability to reason effectively to solve problems is at the heart of critical thinking and problem solving. To understand the problem and pick the best solution, students must understand systems of ideas, which are interrelated concepts that have many components and relationships. All solutions will affect many facets of the system, so students must be able to determine what those relationships and components are and how each will be influenced by a given solution.

To become an effective problem solver, students must

- Ask questions to deepen understanding and gain information about the problem.
- Frame the problem accurately.
- Evaluate information in terms of its usefulness and credibility.
- Analyze information about the problem and potential solutions.
- Explore potential solutions from a variety of viewpoints.
- Evaluate the potential consequences of a proposed solution.
- Select the best solution and put it into action.

Students need to automate the processes involved in thinking critically about information and in solving problems. In developing instruction around these skills, teachers should

- Provide time for students to think through the information for themselves prior to working with others.
- Accept solutions selected by students but push them to reflect on the solutions carefully.
- Encourage students frequently but avoid praise; students should develop intrinsic motivation and learn to trust their own judgment about the value of an idea.
- Provide thoughtful questions that will help students think through the process and reflect on the appropriateness of their decisions.
- Ask students to use multiple perspectives when examining a problem or situation.
- Direct students to consider both intentional and unintentional consequences when adopting a solution.
- Consider using collaborative problem-solving models, in which students work within a group to solve a problem. Provide opportunities for students to reflect on their own behavior within the group and assess how they can work more effectively as group members.

TEACHING COMMUNICATION

The goal of communication is to ensure that the message is understood by the intended audience. Effective communication involves

- Clearly understanding the purpose of the message and the information or idea to be shared.
- Considering the audience and the effect the message may have on them.
- Determining a method of communication, which could include the use of appropriate media and technologies, that would best deliver the message.
- Crafting a message that is clear and consistent with the intended purpose.
- Assessing the potential effect of the message on others.

To work together, students must be able to communicate effectively.

TEACHING COLLABORATION

Effective collaboration is not just about sharing information; it is also about creating new knowledge and understandings. Working together, students often develop better solutions, create new ideas, and think more critically about an issue or concept. The quality of a group's work is influenced by the collaboration skills the members bring to the group.

Effective collaboration involves a host of social and group skills, including the ability to communicate ideas. Students need to see their role as part of the whole, contributing their own ideas while assimilating the ideas of others in order to expand their own knowledge and create a shared body of knowledge with the group.

In addition to monitoring the content students are learning through collaboration, teachers need to provide students with training in the skills they need to work effectively with others. Effective collaborators

- Actively listen to one another, and listen with understanding.
- Assess the effect of their messages on others.
- Work respectfully with others.
- Follow the rules of the group.
- Compromise to reach common goals based on a group's consensus.
- Take responsibility as a member of the team, contributing their fair share of the work.
- Value the ideas, opinions, and work of others.
- Keep an open mind to new ideas, perspectives, and information.
- See things as others see them by paraphrasing ideas.
- Deal with conflict effectively.

To help students learn to become skillful in the art of collaboration, teachers must provide them with ample opportunities to collaborate in meaningful ways about important ideas.

WHY IT'S IMPORTANT TO TEACH THE FOUR CS

Learning is engaging and motivates students to continue to learn. Educators' goal should be to make the learning process visible so that students can reflect on their own learning processes and skills and improve them.

To become proficient and skillful learners and innovators, students need to practice their thinking routines and processes multiple times with different content. They must internalize the thinking processes so that they can efficiently select the best process for a given situation.

This automaticity of thought is accomplished when students have sufficient modeling, guided practice with feedback, and independent practice.

The four Cs help students

- Deepen their understanding of the content.
- Increase interest in the subject.
- Increase retention of key ideas and concepts.
- Develop thinking routines or models.
- Be prepared for a future that we can only imagine.

References

21st Century Fluency Project. (n.d.). *The fluencies*. Retrieved from http://www.21stcenturyfluency .com/fluencies.cfm

Casner-Lotto, J., & Barrington, L. (2006). *Are they really ready to work? Employers' perspectives on the basic knowledge and applied skills of new entrants to the 21st century U.S. workforce*. Retrieved from http:// www.p21.org/documents/FINAL_REPORT_PDF09-29-06.pdf

Costa, A. L. (2008, February). The thought-filled curriculum. *Educational Leadership, 65*(5), 20–24.

Greenspan, A. (2000, April 11). *The evolving demands for skills*. Remarks at the U.S. Department of Labor National Skills Summit, Washington, DC. Retrieved from http://wdr.doleta.gov/research/pdf/ greenspan411.pdf

Kempster Group. (2008, November). *California ICT digital literacy assessments and curriculum framework*. Retrieved from http://www.ictliteracy.info/rf.pdf/California%20ICT%20Assessments%20and%20 Curriculum%20Framework.pdf

Partnership for 21st Century Skills. (2003). *Learning for the 21st century: A report and mile guide for 21st century skills*. Retrieved from http://www.p21.org/images/stories/otherdocs/p21up_Report.pdf

Partnership for 21st Century Skills. (2009). *P21 framework definitions*. Retrieved from http://www .p21.org/documents/P21_Framework_Definitions.pdf

Instructional Planning Tools

Creating a Well-Rounded Set of
   Learning Opportunities

Planning Instructional Design

Sharing the Instructional Plan with Students

Additional Instructional Planning Tools

Creating a Well-Rounded Set of Learning Opportunities

Integrating 21st century skills with academic content can seem overwhelming. Carefully selecting academic content and coupling it with interdisciplinary themes, application, and process skills can help ensure that students have the practice and experience they need to develop the knowledge and skills that will prepare them for their futures.

The Tracking Integration of 21st Century Skills template is designed to help you plan instruction that incorporates 21st century skills. By tracking when you teach the skills, you can help ensure that students have the opportunity to learn and practice the full range of skills and processes.

Not every instructional plan has to include every skill; the goal is to create a well-rounded set of learning opportunities that will help students develop skills in all areas. As you plan instruction, consider how students can become metacognitive about these skills, recognizing when they use them, evaluating their personal levels of success with them, and developing and improving in their use over time.

Tracking Integration of 21st Century Skills

UNIT	Creativity and Innovation	Critical Thinking	Communication	Collaboration	Information Literacy	Media Literacy	ITC Literacy	Flexibility and Adaptability	Initiative and Self-Direction	Social and Cross-Cultural Skills	Productivity and Accountability	Leadership and Responsibility

Instructional Planning

Planning Instructional Design

You can help students understand the subject-area content at deeper and more meaning levels by carefully planning how to meld content with 21st century skills. The following Instructional Design Planner can guide you through that process.

HOW TO USE THIS TOOL

1. Select content.

Choose the content you will teach. The content standards you select will probably come from local or state curriculum standards. In selecting standards to include, consider the following:

- Is this important learning?
- Why is this important for students to learn?
- How can I make this learning important to students? How will I help them see it as useful or relevant?

2. Infuse thematic connections.

Choose the interdisciplinary themes that can be infused with the content. These themes help students see a connection between the subject-area content and broader themes important to life and work in the 21st century. Select only those that logically and closely connect to the content you are teaching. In selecting the themes, consider the following:

- Is there a clear connection between the content and the theme you are selecting?
- How will you draw students' attention to this connection and make it evident to them?

3. Incorporate 21st century skills.

Choose the 21st century skills that you will incorporate into the instructional design. These skills should closely align with the task you create for students. As you think about the task, consider how one or more of these skill categories might fit naturally with the content you are teaching. The skills should be part of the learning and flow from the task.

For example, as you think about the task you will be assigning, consider how students could collaborate on it, what problems they might work on, how you could include technology in the task, or how time management might be a factor. By thinking through the 21st century skills as you design the task, you can better choose tools that would be appropriate. Consider the following:

- What grouping patterns would be appropriate in completing this task?
- How will students evaluate their own skills as a member of a team and in their growth as individuals?
- How will students evaluate their own strengths and areas for growth in using the 21st century skills?
- Is the skill area a logical extension of the content?
- How will infusing the selected skills extend and refine students' learning about the content?

4. Define the learning task.

Define the task that students will perform. The task should both help students understand the content standard and provide practice in implementing the selected 21st century skills. Consider clearly delineating both the content standard and the 21st century skills in the task when you present it to students. Guiding questions for task creation include

- Is the product I am asking students to produce going to result in long-term learning?
- How will I evaluate diverse responses and thinking?
- What options will students have for communicating their learning or understanding?
- How will I help students recognize both the content standard and the 21st century skill they are learning?
- Does the task directly relate to the learning I am hoping to facilitate?
- Is the task meaningful, relevant, and interesting to students?

5. Select instructional tools.

Select the instructional tools you will use in the task. The chart on pages 46–49 will help direct you to some specific tools that address various skills. For example, if you have selected "communication" as a skill embedded in the task, you might refer to the chart to find a variety of tools that can help teach this skill.

Because the tools are generic, you can use them with virtually any content area or task. You can also use the tools as they are presented or modify them to meet the specific needs of the task. In selecting tools, consider the following:

- Does the tool match the learning outcomes of the task?
- What modifications to the tool would make it a better match to the desired learning?
- Over the course of several instructional tasks, have the selected tools covered a broad range of 21st century skills?

6. Develop assessments.

Determine how you will assess student learning with the task. Consider offering students multiple options for demonstrating their learning and achievement. Be sure to share what success on this task will look like before beginning instruction. Students need a clear target for their learning. As you plan for assessment, think about

- What is acceptable as evidence that students have achieved the learning?
- How can I differentiate assessments by providing multiple options to students?
- How will I make students aware of the expectations for learning and performance?
- Is there a rubric or performance indicator that I can use to clarify expectations and set clear targets for performance?

7. Plan for metacognition.

Describe how students will become aware of the 21st century skills incorporated into the task. Students must be metacognitive about the skills they are learning. They should be able to identify the skills when they use them, be able to evaluate their personal levels of success in using them, and be aware of their development and improvement across time.

In thinking about how to help students be aware of the 21st century skills embedded in the task, consider the following:

- Can students identify the 21st century skills they are applying in the task?
- What questions could you ask to lead students to an understanding of these skills?
- How can you help students monitor their use of the skills and improve on them?
- Can students identify how they can use these skill sets with different content or apply them to various aspects of their lives?

After you have completed an instructional plan, use the checklist Reflecting on the Instructional Plan on page 35 to evaluate how well you have incorporated each of these important elements in instruction.

Planning Instructional Design

Instructional Design Planner

Topic: _____

Dates: _____

Content Standard

What will students know, be able to do, or understand at the completion of this instruction?

Instructional Planning

Interdisciplinary Theme

Which themes can be infused with the content?

- ☐ Global awareness
- ☐ Financial, economic, business, and entrepreneurial literacy
- ☐ Civic literacy
- ☐ Health literacy
- ☐ Environmental literacy

21st Century Skills

Which skills will be incorporated in the instructional design?

Learning and Innovation Skills	Information, Media, and Technology Skills	Life and Career Skills
☐ Creativity and Innovation ☐ Critical Thinking and Problem Solving ☐ Communication ☐ Collaboration	☐ Information Literacy ☐ Media Literacy ☐ Information, Communications, and Technology Literacy	☐ Flexibility and Adaptability ☐ Initiative and Self-Direction ☐ Social and Cross-Cultural Skills ☐ Productivity and Accountability ☐ Leadership and Responsibility

Task Description

What task or tasks will you ask students to perform?

Tools to Use

Which tools will you use in this instructional plan?

Name of Tool	Page	Name of Tool	Page

Assessment

How will you evaluate student learning? What options will you provide for demonstrating learning?

Skill Awareness

How will students become aware of their own use of the 21st century skills? What questions will you use for reflection and discussion?

Reflecting on the Instructional Plan

After you have completed an instructional plan, take a few moments to reflect on whether it meets the key characteristics below. Place a check mark in front of those that the plan addresses.

√	Characteristic
Select Content	
	The content is important for students to learn.
	I can explain to students why the learning goals are important.
	I have planned for how to make this content important to students and help them see it as useful and relevant.
Infuse Thematic Connections	
	There is a clear connection between the content and the theme I am selecting.
	I have a plan for how to draw students' attention to this connection and make it evident to them.
Incorporate 21st Century Skills	
	I will use appropriate grouping patterns to teach the 21st century skills.
	Students will evaluate their own skills as a member of a team and their growth in collaborative skills.
	The 21st century skills I selected are a logical extension of the content.
	The 21st century skills I selected will extend and refine students' learning about the content.
Define the Learning Task	
	The product I am asking students to produce will result in long-term learning.
	I have a plan for evaluating the diverse responses and thinking of students.
	Students have options for communicating their learning and understanding.
	Students will be able to identify both the content standard and the 21st century skills they are learning.
	The task directly relates to the targeted learning.
	The task is meaningful, relevant, and interesting to students.

Instructional Planning

Instructional Planning

√	Characteristic
Select Instructional Tools	
	The tools I selected match the learning outcomes of the task.
	I've modified the tool as necessary to match the intended learning from the task.
	The selected tools represent a broad range of 21st century skills.
Develop Assessments	
	The assessments will provide clear evidence that students have achieved the desired learning.
	I have differentiated assessments by providing multiple options for students to demonstrate their mastery of the content.
	I've made students aware of the expectations for learning and performance.
	A rubric or performance indicators clarify expectations and set clear targets for performance.
Plan for Metacognition	
	Students will be able to identify the 21st century skills they are using to carry out the task.
	I have developed questions that will lead students to understanding the 21st century skills.
	Students will evaluate their own strengths and areas for growth in the use of the 21st century skills.
	I have included activities that help students monitor and improve their use of the 21st century skills.
	Students can identify how they can use the 21st century skills with different content or apply them to various aspects of their lives or futures.

Sharing the Instructional Plan with Students

The Instructional Design Planner on page 33 is designed for teacher reflection and planning. But for instruction to have its greatest effect, we also have to make sure that students understand our expectations and plans so that they, too, have a blueprint for learning.

To help you create clear targets for learning and performance, fill out the following instructional planning template, Learning Plan, and share it with students. It's best to share the completed template with students at the beginning of instruction, much like giving out a course syllabus at the beginning of an academic course.

Much of the contents of the Learning Plan will come directly from the Instructional Design Planner. If you will be using rubrics, graphic organizers, tools, reflection sheets, and so forth during this instructional period, consider attaching them to the student plan. The goal of the planner is to ensure complete communication with students about your expectations and to create clear targets for student learning and performance.

HOW TO USE THIS TOOL

You can customize the Learning Plan template to match the needs of the content and instruction. The most important thing is to ensure that the plan provides students with a clear and thorough picture of what they will be learning (content and skill expectations) and what they will be expected to do to demonstrate that learning (assessment). The plan must also clearly define the tasks and tools that will help them reach the learning targets.

A brief description of each component of the template is below.

Component	Description
Learning Focus	A brief and clear description of what students will know, be able to do, or understand as a result of successfully completing this learning plan.
21st Century Skills	The categories of skills that students will use or you will teach. This will help students learn the language of the 21st century skills. It is important to engage students in understanding how they can apply these skills effectively.

Instructional Planning

Sharing the Instructional Plan with Students

Component	Description
Task Description	An overview of the tasks that the student will be asked to complete to fulfill the requirements of the learning plan.
Tools to Use	A list of the tools that students will be required to use in demonstrating completion of the learning task. If students have a choice in the tools they can use, that should be indicated. Students might also be encouraged to create their own tools or modify the suggested ones.
Evaluating My Learning	An overview of how the students will be evaluated and held accountable for both content and process in their performance.
Thinking About My Learning	Questions for reflection and discussion. These questions should reflect the "Skills Awareness" component of the Instructional Design Planner.

Learning Plan

Topic: _____

Dates: _____

Learning Focus
What will I know, be able to do, or understand?

21st Century Skills
Which skills will I be applying to this learning?

Learning and Innovation Skills	Information, Media, and Technology Skills	Life and Career Skills
☐ Creativity and Innovation ☐ Critical Thinking and Problem Solving ☐ Communication ☐ Collaboration	☐ Information Literacy ☐ Media Literacy ☐ Information, Communications, and Technology Literacy	☐ Flexibility and Adaptability ☐ Initiative and Self-Direction ☐ Social and Cross-Cultural Skills ☐ Productivity and Accountability ☐ Leadership and Responsibility

Task Description
What task or tasks will I be performing?

Instructional Planning

Instructional Planning

Tools to Use

Which tools will I use in learning?

Evaluating My Learning

How will my learning and performance be evaluated?

Thinking About My Learning

Questions to use in reflecting on my learning and the thinking processes I used in this lesson.

Additional Instructional Planning Tools

The Instructional Design Planner (see page 33) and its student version, the Learning Plan (see page 39), provide a comprehensive format for thinking through how to infuse content-area learning with 21st century skills. There isn't one best approach to planning instruction for this purpose. The key is the conscientious process of thinking about how you can present both content and 21st century skills as students learn about a given topic or learn a content skill.

For example, if students were learning about ecosystems,

- You could present a problem-solving activity (critical thinking) that asks students to determine what would happen if one of the elements of that system were to disappear.
- Students could then work in groups (collaboration) to complete a graphic organizer that demonstrates the results (creativity).
- They could share their collaborative thinking by creating a document, a visual or media presentation, or a speech (communication and possibly technology).

In this scenario, the emphasis is still primarily on learning the about ecosystems—the content—but students have also used 21st century learning skills in the process. At the end of the unit or lesson, students need to reflect not only on what they have learned, but also on how they have learned it.

The following are two more examples of instructional planning tools that you could use in designing and implementing learning opportunities that integrate content with 21st century learning skills.

Instructional Planning

Instructional Planning

Planning Instruction to Integrate 21st Century Skills

Topic: _____

Date(s): _____

Content and skill learning targets:

Learning and Innovation Skills	Tools
Creativity and Innovation Using information and knowledge in new situations or to create new knowledge.	
Critical Thinking and Problem Solving Using reasoning, analytical thinking, and knowledge to solve problems or evaluate information.	
Communication Articulating thoughts, ideas, and information orally, in writing, or in visual or auditory presentations.	
Collaboration Working with others to create new ideas, share information, or learn from each other.	
Information, Communications, and Technology Literacy	**Tools**
Selecting and using appropriate technology to accomplish the task.	
Life and Career Skills	**Tools**
Holding students accountable for their learning and for taking personal responsibility for their work.	
Metacognition and Reflection	**Activities**
How students will reflect on the effectiveness of their own learning processes.	

Additional Instructional Planning Tools

Curriculum Snapshot for Creating Learning Opportunities

Topic: _____

Date(s): _____

21st Century Skills Integrated	Content Learning Targets	Metacognitive Strategies (Questions for reflection on the learning)
☐ Creativity ☐ Critical Thinking ☐ Communication ☐ Collaboration ☐ Information Literacy ☐ Media Literacy ☐ Information, Communications, and Technology Literacy ☐ Life and Career Skills		

Instructional Plan	Assessment Strategies
Before Instruction: During Instruction: After Instruction:	
Resources Needed:	

Classroom Tools for Students

Selecting the Classroom Tools

Creating Your Own 21st Century Tools

Selecting the Classroom Tools

The following chart provides guidance about which categories of 21st century skills each tool addresses. Depending on how the teacher's instructional choices, the integration of media literacy; information, communication, and technology literacy; and life and career skills may vary.

Tools	Learning and Innovation Skills				Information Literacy	Page
	Creativity and Innovation	**Critical Thinking and Problem Solving**	**Communication**	**Collaboration**	**Information Literacy**	
	• Think creatively. • Work creatively with others. • Implement innovations.	• Reason effectively. • Use systems thinking. • Make judgments and decisions. • Solve problems.	• Communicate clearly.	• Collaborate with others.	• Access and evaluate information. • Use and manage information.	**Page**
20 Questions	X	X				50
A Dime a Time		X	X	X		53
Based on the Facts		X			X	56
Beginnings and Endings with Muscle	X		X	X	X	59
Big Ideas		X		X	X	62
Breaking It Down		X	X		X	65
Coloring Our Knowledge	X	X	X	X		68
Converging Ideas		X	X		X	71
Convince Me!		X	X		X	74
Connect, Summarize, and Ask	X	X	X		X	77
Creating Good Questions	X	X	X	X		80

Classroom Tools

Selecting the Classroom Tools

Tools	Learning and Innovation Skills				Information Literacy	Page
	Creativity and Innovation	Critical Thinking and Problem Solving	Communication	Collaboration		
	• Think creatively. • Work creatively with others. • Implement innovations.	• Reason effectively. • Use systems thinking. • Make judgments and decisions. • Solve problems.	• Communicate clearly.	• Collaborate with others.	• Access and evaluate information. • Use and manage information.	
Decision Tree	X	X	X	X	X	84
Developing Consensus	X	X	X	X		87
Evaluating My Own Understanding		X			X	92
Four Corners		X	X	X		96
Framing the Problem		X			X	100
Ground Rules for Teams			X	X		103
I'm Sure of It… or Not		X	X			106
Investigation by Three		X	X	X	X	109
Learn, Discuss, and Summarize		X	X	X	X	112
Making Good Decisions	X	X	X	X		115
My Action Plan		X	X		X	119
Our Shared Learning	X	X	X	X		123
Picking the Right Site		X	X	X	X	127
Planning My Learning	X	X			X	130
Point, Counterpoint		X	X	X		135

Classroom Tools

Selecting the Classroom Tools

Tools	Learning and Innovation Skills				Information Literacy	Page
	Creativity and Innovation	Critical Thinking and Problem Solving	Communication	Collaboration		
	• Think creatively. • Work creatively with others. • Implement innovations.	• Reason effectively. • Use systems thinking. • Make judgments and decisions. • Solve problems.	• Communicate clearly.	• Collaborate with others.	• Access and evaluate information. • Use and manage information.	
Preparing, Engaging, and Applying My Learning	X	X				138
Processing the Data	X	X	X		X	142
Putting It into Perspective		X	X	X		145
Questioning the Topic	X	X			X	148
Questions in Search of Answers		X	X	X	X	151
Reflecting on My Learning		X			X	154
Remote Control Thinking	X		X		X	157
Respecting Different Perspectives		X	X	X		162
Round-Robin Ideas	X	X	X	X		165
Support It and Share It		X	X	X	X	169
Supporting Evidence		X	X	X	X	172
The Pros and Cons		X	X	X	X	175
The Viewpoint		X	X	X	X	178

Classroom Tools

Tools	Learning and Innovation Skills				Information Literacy	Page
	Creativity and Innovation	Critical Thinking and Problem Solving	Communication	Collaboration		
	• Think creatively. • Work creatively with others. • Implement innovations.	• Reason effectively. • Use systems thinking. • Make judgments and decisions. • Solve problems.	• Communicate clearly.	• Collaborate with others.	• Access and evaluate information. • Use and manage information.	
Think Before You Judge	X	X	X	X	X	181
Three-by-Three Research		X	X		X	185
Using Primary Sources		X	X		X	188
Weighing Consequences	X	X	X			192
Working Together Rubric			X	X		195

Classroom Tools

20 Questions

Learning and Innovation Skills	Information, Media, and Technology Skills	Life and Career Skills (Check those to be addressed)
✓ Creativity and Innovation ✓ Critical Thinking and Problem Solving ○ Communication ○ Collaboration	○ Information Literacy ○ Media Literacy ○ Information, Communications, and Technology Literacy	☐ Flexibility and Adaptability ☐ Initiative and Self-Direction ☐ Social and Cross-Cultural Skills ☐ Productivity and Accountability ☐ Leadership and Responsibility

The questions in this tool can help students develop new ideas or ways of thinking about a situation or problem they are studying.

HOW TO USE THIS TOOL

1. Identify an idea or idea that you want to have students understand and think creatively about.

2. Review in class the 20 question stems in the chart to ensure that students understand what each means.

3. Students select three of the questions to use in the activity. They should enter the number of the questions they chose in the left-hand column.

4. Students use each question to develop new ideas or ways of thinking about the overall idea and provide suggestions in the "Ideas" column.

5. After processing each of the three questions, students complete the summary statement at the bottom of the page. They should be prepared to share their ideas with a small group or the whole class.

TIPS FOR USING THIS TOOL

• Be sure that students have enough background knowledge about the overall idea before they start the activity.

• Model the process with a topic or idea with which students are already familiar.

• Students can work through the process individually or in small groups.

• After students are familiar with this process, encourage them to develop additional questions that will help them think creatively about the topic or idea.

• Have students select a specific idea and further develop it into a presentation to share with others.

USING TECHNOLOGY

• Create a collaborative online document that includes all of the questions, with spaces for responses after each one. Ask students to contribute ideas for any or all of the questions. They can build on one another's ideas or add new suggestions.

• Have students conduct an Internet search on the topic or idea to gather more background information. (See "Picking the Right Site" on page 127 to teach students about Internet searches.)

• Set up a blog, Twitter account, or other online sharing tool that students can use to have an online dialogue about various ideas or suggestions.

THINKING IT THROUGH

You can address these questions during class discussion, in small groups, in student journals, or in a variety of other ways.

• What is the value of looking at ideas in different ways? Give an example of how you could apply this process in your life.

• Explain why you picked the questions you did. What was your rationale for each one?

• How did using the questions help you think creatively about the original idea?

• Was the final idea better than the original one? Why or why not?

Classroom Tools

20 Questions

When seeking new ideas, it is sometimes helpful to look at the situation or the problem by asking questions that help us think about it in new ways.

1. Select at least three of the following questions and then apply them to the situation or problem you are studying.
2. Write your answers in the space below the questions.
3. Summarize your thinking at the bottom of the page.

Idea: _____

Questions	
1. What if…? 2. How can we improve…? 3. How will others benefit? 4. What are we forgetting? 5. What's the next step? 6. What can we do better? 7. What do you think about…? 8. How can we improve the quality of…? 9. How can we streamline…? 10. How can we modify it?	11. What could we replace? 12. What could we add? 13. What could we eliminate? 14. What might be changing about this? 15. What will make it work? 16. What other ideas do you have? 17. What issues does this create? 18. What patterns do we see? 19. How can we simplify it? 20. Why do this?
Potential Answers	
Question #	**Ideas**

IN SUMMARY

We can improve the idea by…

A Dime a Time

Learning and Innovation Skills	Information, Media, and Technology Skills	Life and Career Skills (Check those to be addressed)
○ Creativity and Innovation ✓ Critical Thinking and Problem Solving ✓ Communication ✓ Collaboration	○ Information Literacy ○ Media Literacy ○ Information, Communications, and Technology Literacy	☐ Flexibility and Adaptability ☐ Initiative and Self-Direction ☐ Social and Cross-Cultural Skills ☐ Productivity and Accountability ☐ Leadership and Responsibility

This tool can help students understand the importance of choosing the right words to share ideas clearly and precisely. The tool also gives students an opportunity to practice summarizing key ideas and writing concise sentences.

HOW TO USE THIS TOOL

1. Discuss the need to be concise in summarizing ideas. Have students describe what the word *concise* means and why this is important in communicating ideas.
2. After students have learned about a topic, they develop a series of summary sentences that present the key points about the topic.
3. Explain that students have a budget of $10 for their summary sentences. Each sentence costs a flat rate of 50 cents, plus each word in that sentence costs an additional 10 cents. For example, a sentence with eight words would cost 50 cents for the sentence and 80 cents for the eight words, for a total of $1.30.
4. After completing their summary sentences, students total up the amount they have spent and share their sentences in small groups or with the class as a whole.

TIPS FOR USING THIS TOOL

• Using text or information from a previous unit, model how to develop concise summary statements.

• Remind students that sentences must express complete thoughts. It may be helpful to review what constitutes a complete sentence.

• After the activity, ask students to expand their ideas with more details.

• Students can use their sentence summaries to create a presentation on the main ideas of the topic.

Classroom Tools

• Have small groups of students share their sentence summaries, analyzing them for common themes or ideas.

USING TECHNOLOGY

• Each sentence summary can form the foundation for a separate PowerPoint slide. Encourage students to use graphic elements in their slides. You can combine slides created by individual students or pairs with those from other students to form a single presentation about the topic.

• Compare writing brief summary statements to text messaging. Discuss how the two are alike and different.

THINKING IT THROUGH

You can address these questions during class discussion, in small groups, in student journals, or in a variety of other ways.

• What is most difficult about expressing an idea in a few words?

• Give examples of when it might be important to be able to share information briefly and concisely.

• Describe the thinking process you used to determine the most important points to include in your list. How did you determine what was important or not important?

• Review your list of summary sentences. As a whole, do they capture the most important points? Explain why you think they do or do not.

Classroom Tools

A Dime a Time

Choosing the right words is important in sharing ideas clearly and precisely. Write a summary of what you have learned about the topic. Each word costs 10 cents, and each sentence costs 50 cents. You have a total of $10 to spend on your summary of the topic.

Write each sentence of your summary in a row below and total its cost in the column on the right.

Summary Sentence	Cost ($.50 + $.10 per word)

Total Cost: _____

Classroom Tools

Based on the Facts

Learning and Innovation Skills	Information, Media, and Technology Skills	Life and Career Skills (Check those to be addressed)
○ Creativity and Innovation ✓ Critical Thinking and Problem Solving ○ Communication ○ Collaboration	✓ Information Literacy ○ Media Literacy ○ Information, Communications, and Technology Literacy	☐ Flexibility and Adaptability ☐ Initiative and Self-Direction ☐ Social and Cross-Cultural Skills ☐ Productivity and Accountability ☐ Leadership and Responsibility

This tool gives students practice in gathering facts, as distinguished from opinions, about a topic that they can use as a factual basis for solving a problem or generalizing a concept.

HOW TO USE THIS TOOL

1. Ask students what they already know about the topic they will be studying.
2. Describe the difference between a fact and an opinion. Provide students with examples to help them understand the difference.
3. Explain that the purpose of this activity is to gather facts about the topic.
4. Students read the assigned material, listen to a presentation, or view a video about the topic.
5. As they learn about the topic, students list all the facts, evaluating each to ensure that it is a fact and not an opinion.
6. Using the facts they have accumulated, students formulate a generalization, prediction, or opinion.

TIPS FOR USING THIS TOOL

• It may be helpful to model using facts to create a generalization, prediction, or opinion.
• Students might work in pairs to develop their lists.
• Consider providing frequent breaks in the presentation of information to allow students to note the facts they are learning.
• You can conduct the activity in reverse, presenting the generalization, prediction, or opinion before students locate the facts that support it.
• If students gather facts from more than one source, they should record the source of each fact.

• All students can use the same sources of information, or they can use different sources for identifying facts.

• You or the students can identify the sources of information. If students are charged with finding sources, brainstorm ways to identify sources and ask students to explain why their sources would be appropriate.

USING TECHNOLOGY

• Use the Internet to locate sources of information. Remind students to check the credibility of their sources before using them (see "Picking the Right Site" on page 127).

• Post all of the facts on a website, wiki, or collaborative online tool that allows students to see one another's ideas. Then ask students to work in small groups to develop generalizations, predictions, or opinions.

• Ask students to create a short media presentation to share their findings.

THINKING IT THROUGH

You can address these questions during class discussion, in small groups, in student journals, or in a variety of other ways.

• How did you determine what was a fact versus what was opinion?

• How could you double-check facts if you were unsure?

• Describe your thinking as you arrived at your conclusion. Which facts were most influential in your thinking process?

• Do you think your own biases or opinions influenced the facts you selected? Why or why not?

Classroom Tools

  57

Based on the Facts

List several facts you have gathered about the topic, and identify the source of each fact. Review the facts and develop a generalization, prediction, or opinion based on them.

Topic: _____

Fact	Source

GENERALIZATION, PREDICTION, OR OPINION

Beginnings and Endings with Muscle

Learning and Innovation Skills	Information, Media, and Technology Skills	Life and Career Skills (Check those to be addressed)
✓ Creativity and Innovation ○ Critical Thinking and Problem Solving ✓ Communication ✓ Collaboration	✓ Information Literacy ✓ Media Literacy ○ Information, Communications, and Technology Literacy	☐ Flexibility and Adaptability ☐ Initiative and Self-Direction ☐ Social and Cross-Cultural Skills ☐ Productivity and Accountability ☐ Leadership and Responsibility

This tool helps students understand the importance of a strong introduction and conclusion in a written work, presentation, or speech in capturing the audience's attention and leaving a lasting impression. It also gives students various methods for practicing writing effective introductions and conclusions.

HOW TO USE THIS TOOL

1. Discuss the need for effective introductions and conclusions when creating a presentation or when writing.
2. Students brainstorm the kinds of things that constitute powerful introductions and conclusions and give examples of strong introductions or conclusions that left lasting impressions on them.
3. For the given topic, students work alone or in small groups to create ideas for potential introductions and conclusions for each method on the graphic organizer. If students have identified additional methods, they can add them to the list.
4. Students select the ideas they think are most effective and use one for the introduction and one for the conclusion of a presentation on the topic.

TIPS FOR USING THIS TOOL

• Help students understand the importance of considering the audience in creating their introductions and conclusions. What will capture their attention? How will they leave a lasting impression?

• Students don't have to completely flesh out their ideas for this activity. The goal is to have them view in a variety of ways the concept that they are trying to communicate. Once students have chosen the approach they are going to use, they can plan a more thorough implementation of it.

Classroom Tools

• Consider finding video clips, written passages, or speeches that have powerful beginnings and endings. Ask students to react to these in terms of what caught their interest or left an impression.

USING TECHNOLOGY

• Listen to or view the introductions and conclusions of famous speeches, and ask students to evaluate the effect these had on the audience.
• Have students create a video presentation on the topic using both audio and visual elements.

THINKING IT THROUGH

You can address these questions during class discussion, in small groups, in student journals, or in a variety of other ways.

• What captures your attention when listening to a speaker or watching a video? How do you decide if you want to continue to listen or watch?
• Which method for creating a strong introduction or conclusion was easiest for you to develop? Which was most difficult? Why?
• Explain why you chose the introduction and conclusion you used in your presentation.
• Do you think your introduction and conclusion effectively communicated your message? Why or why not?

Classroom Tools

Beginnings and Endings with Muscle

Strong introductions and conclusions make a piece of writing, a presentation, or a speech more memorable.

1. Select a Topic: _____

2. For the topic you have selected, write either an introduction or conclusion using each of the suggestions below.

Method	Introduction or Conclusion
1. Raise a question that gets the attention of the audience.	
2. Share something that the character or person does that is out of the ordinary.	
3. Get inside the head of one of the characters or people by sharing their thoughts.	
4. Make an exclamatory statement that expresses a strong emotion.	
5. Share a strong opinion or point of view.	
6. Use a quote from one of the characters or a famous person.	
7. Help the audience create a picture in their minds with a vivid description.	

3. Select the introduction and conclusion that you think will be most effective in presenting your topic and use it in your presentation.

Classroom Tools

 # Big Ideas

Learning and Innovation Skills	Information, Media, and Technology Skills	Life and Career Skills (Check those to be addressed)
○ Creativity and Innovation ✓ Critical Thinking and Problem Solving ○ Communication ✓ Collaboration	✓ Information Literacy ○ Media Literacy ○ Information, Communications, and Technology Literacy	☐ Flexibility and Adaptability ☐ Initiative and Self-Direction ☐ Social and Cross-Cultural Skills ☐ Productivity and Accountability ☐ Leadership and Responsibility

This tool can help students learn how to identify the major parts, or big ideas, of a topic they are studying.

HOW TO USE THIS TOOL

1. Conduct a class discussion on what constitutes a *big idea*, which is an idea or concept that can be broken down into many details or components. Model identifying big ideas on common subjects.

2. Students brainstorm some big ideas on the topic being studied. They might get clues from headings and subheadings in text or on websites. Students write these big ideas in the first column of the graphic organizer.

3. Students enter details, explanations, or examples for each big idea in the second column, using key words and phrases rather than whole sentences. This information can come from their research, a reading assignment, a video, or a presentation on the topic.

4. Pairs of students can share their lists prior to a whole-class discussion.

TIPS FOR USING THIS TOOL

• Prior to instruction, ask students to predict what they think will be the big ideas about the topic.

• If you are using a text, have students do a 90-second scan of the text to look for main ideas and key words and phrases.

• Consider framing the big ideas as questions rather than subtopics.

• You can break students into small groups to complete the details, explanations, and examples for each big idea. To ensure that all students are participating, require students to take turns adding suggestions for additions.

- Post the big ideas on chart paper, and allow students to post ideas under each big idea.

USING TECHNOLOGY

- The big ideas students generate can serve as key words in an Internet search.
- Students can use notes from online sources. If they are using multiple sources or are allowed to search for their own sources, they should cite the URL or website from which they obtained the information.
- Have students pool ideas using Google Docs or another online collaboration tool. Students can then search through the generated ideas, looking for commonalities or patterns in the information—the big ideas.

THINKING IT THROUGH

You can address these questions during class discussion, in small groups, in student journals, or in a variety of other ways.

- How might your background experiences or culture affect what you consider important about a topic?
- What criteria did you use in classifying something as a big idea as opposed to a detail?
- What did you find easy or difficult about identifying big ideas?
- Why is being able to identify big ideas an important skill? When can you use this skill in other ways?

Classroom Tools

Big Ideas

1. Summarize the big ideas, or major parts, of the topic you are studying and enter them in the "Big Ideas" column.
2. Enter supporting details, explanations, and examples in the second column using key words and phrases.

Big Ideas	Details, Explanations, and Examples

Breaking It Down

Learning and Innovation Skills	Information, Media, and Technology Skills	Life and Career Skills (Check those to be addressed)
○ Creativity and Innovation ✓ Critical Thinking and Problem Solving ✓ Communication ○ Collaboration	✓ Information Literacy ○ Media Literacy ○ Information, Communications, and Technology Literacy	☐ Flexibility and Adaptability ☐ Initiative and Self-Direction ☐ Social and Cross-Cultural Skills ☐ Productivity and Accountability ☐ Leadership and Responsibility

This tool can help students better understand a topic they're studying by breaking it down into subtopics or smaller components. It also provides an opportunity for them to practice gathering information from a text.

HOW TO USE THIS TOOL

1. Enter into the graphic organizer

   • The topic or concept students will be examining.

   • The categories or subtopics related to the topic or concept. You could ask students to help develop the subtopics.

2. Students collect details, examples, and supporting information for each category, using resources that you provide or ones they locate, and note those under the appropriate subtopic.

3. When students have explored all four subtopics, they review the notes in each subtopic and write a short summary about what is important to remember about the overall topic or concept.

TIPS FOR USING THIS TOOL

• Model how to use text or graphic features to identify subtopics or categories. Ask students to quickly scan the headings, subheadings, boldfaced words, suggested alternative search words, pictures, charts, and so forth to look for repeated ideas that suggest main subtopics or categories. This can be done with printed text or electronic text.

• If students' prior knowledge about the topic is low, ask them to think logically about the topic and predict what they think important subtopics, components, or headings might be.

• Ask students to brainstorm a list of potential words or phrases that they could use in an online search on the topic.

• Students can use the graphic organizer as the springboard for a presentation, written essay, or visual summary of the topic.

USING TECHNOLOGY

• Ask students to compare the text features found in websites with the text features found in printed materials (headings, subheadings, pictures, captions, graphs, charts, boldfaced words, etc.). Ask them to compile a list of suggestions for reading on the web.

• Allow students to use a wide variety of presentation tools to present their findings to the class. Ask them to reflect on how the tool they chose affected the audience's attention, interest, or understanding of the information (see "Beginnings and Endings with Muscle" on page 59).

THINKING IT THROUGH

You can address these questions during class discussion, in small groups, in student journals, or in a variety of other ways.

• Describe the thinking process you used to determine the subtopics or components.

• Does breaking down the topic into parts make it easier to understand? Why or why not?

• How does using subtopics help you become more efficient in gathering information?

• Describe how you chose the information that was included in your summary.

Breaking It Down

Locate information that supports each subtopic, and note it in the appropriate boxes.

Topic: _____

Subtopic:	**Subtopic:**
Subtopic:	**Subtopic:**

SUMMARY

Use information from all four subtopics to write a two- to three-sentence summary of what is most important to remember about the topic or concept.

 # Coloring Our Knowledge

Learning and Innovation Skills	Information, Media, and Technology Skills	Life and Career Skills (Check those to be addressed)
✓ Creativity and Innovation ✓ Critical Thinking and Problem Solving ✓ Communication ✓ Collaboration	○ Information Literacy ○ Media Literacy ○ Information, Communications, and Technology Literacy	☐ Flexibility and Adaptability ☐ Initiative and Self-Direction ☐ Social and Cross-Cultural Skills ☐ Productivity and Accountability ☐ Leadership and Responsibility

In this tool, students work together to summarize their knowledge about a topic and its importance.

HOW TO USE THIS TOOL

1. Divide the class into small groups, and provide each group with a topic or subtopic related to the concept being studied.

2. Each group appoints a recorder who writes down the group's collaborative answers to each of the questions on the graphic organizer in a colored ink or pencil that is specific to that group. (The color-coding keeps track of which group contributes which comments.)

3. After a given period of time, stop the group discussion and recording and direct the groups to rotate their papers to the next group.

4. On receiving a new graphic organizer, each group reflects on the new subtopic, reviews the previous group's work, and adds information or ideas.

5. Continue to rotate the topics until every group has worked with every subtopic.

6. Return the collective responses to the originating group, which reviews all of the input from the other groups and adds any remaining ideas.

7. If necessary, the original group can ask other groups for clarification about their contributions.

TIPS FOR USING THIS TOOL

• Model the use of the tool as a review of a previous topic that the students have studied.

• At the completion of the activity, groups can create a presentation that incorporates the ideas that the class generated.

- You can use the resulting compilations to gather feedback about how well students have learned the topic and pinpoint any common misconceptions. Then, help students correct any misconceptions or extend their learning through class discussions.
- You can conduct the activity as a gallery walk, with students posting their responses on chart paper as they move in groups around the room.
- Students can rotate the organizer within a single group, with individuals using different colors to record their contributions.

USING TECHNOLOGY

- You can load the questions into an online collaboration tool and have groups input their ideas under each question using a designated font color.
- The documents students created can be posted to a website for use as a review and for further discussion and clarification.
- Create a blog post for each subtopic where students can enter their ideas for each question.

THINKING IT THROUGH

You can address these questions during class discussion, in small groups, in student journals, or in a variety of other ways.

- How does thinking about what you already know about the topic help you understand it?
- Which question was most difficult for you to answer? Why?
- How did you use the ideas of others to create new ideas or to think about the topic in new ways? Give an example.
- Evaluate your contributions to the group's work and your performance as a member of the group. How would you rate yourself as a group member? Give examples to support your self-evaluation. (Note: Consider the Working Together Rubric on page 195 to help students evaluate their contributions.)

Classroom Tools

 69

Coloring Our Knowledge

Each small group will receive one topic related to the subject you have been studying. You will have a few minutes to respond as a group to each of the three questions below. Designate one person to act as a recorder to write down your responses in a unique color.

When the teacher calls "stop," rotate papers with another group, who will add its ideas in a different color. We'll continue the rotations continue until your original paper is returned to your group.

Topic: _____

1. What facts do you know about the topic?

2. What examples or applications can you identify regarding the topic?

3. Why is it important to learn about this topic?

Converging Ideas

Learning and Innovation Skills	Information, Media, and Technology Skills	Life and Career Skills (Check those to be addressed)
○ Creativity and Innovation ✓ Critical Thinking and Problem Solving ✓ Communication ○ Collaboration	✓ Information Literacy ○ Media Literacy ○ Information, Communications, and Technology Literacy	☐ Flexibility and Adaptability ☐ Initiative and Self-Direction ☐ Social and Cross-Cultural Skills ☐ Productivity and Accountability ☐ Leadership and Responsibility

In this tool, students practice drawing conclusions from two different sources that may have conflicting or divergent information.

HOW TO USE THIS TOOL

1. Either provide students, or have them locate on their own, two sources of information for a narrow topic of study.
2. Provide students with a clear purpose for their review of the information.
3. Students read or view each source and take notes on what they believe is important information relevant to the purpose they have been given.
4. Students use information from both sources to create summary statements or conclusions about the topic. Conclusions can be based on common ideas or on discrepancies or conflicts in the information.

TIPS FOR USING THIS TOOL

• Consider modeling the activity with two sources of information familiar to students or with information from a previous unit of instruction.

• Make sure you have sufficiently narrowed down the topic if students are finding their own sources of information. If they are using the Internet to locate information, consider providing them with key search words or phrases, or determine those as a class.

• If students are finding their own sources of information, remind them of the importance of evaluating the sources for reliability. (See "Picking the Right Site" on page 127 for guidelines about reliability of websites.)

• You can establish a minimum number of conclusions that students must draw.

• Students can work in pairs to draw their conclusions from both sources of information.

- Have two pairs of students complete the graphic organizer, with each taking notes from a different source. After the pairs complete their notes and conclusions, tape the two tables together (or copy and paste into a Word document) and have the two pairs of students draw further conclusions based on all four sources.
- You can have different groups of students process different sources of information. Each group then shares their conclusions, and students can compile a master list of important ideas or conclusions.

USING TECHNOLOGY

- Provide students with selected URLs that are of high quality.
- Provide guidance to students on how to determine the validity of information from an online source. Consider using the tool on page 127 or have students create their own list of criteria for judging the credibility of a website.
- Cut and paste excerpts from online sources into a document for students to use as a source.
- Use a shared document website, such as Google Docs, to have students enter and then share their learning and conclusions.

THINKING IT THROUGH

You can address these questions during class discussion, in small groups, in student journals, or in a variety of other ways.

- If you encountered differences in information between sources, how did you decide which one was more credible?
- What criteria did you use to choose the most important points or information to include in your conclusions? What made some information seem more important?
- Did others come to different conclusions than you? Why might that have happened?

Classroom Tools

Converging Ideas

Consider two sources of information on the topic and note important information from each in the top two columns. Use information from both sources to develop summary conclusions in the bottom box.

Topic: _____

Notes from Source 1	Notes from Source 2

Conclusions or Most Important Ideas

Convince Me!

Learning and Innovation Skills	Information, Media, and Technology Skills	Life and Career Skills (Check those to be addressed)
○ Creativity and Innovation ✓ Critical Thinking and Problem Solving ✓ Communication ○ Collaboration	✓ Information Literacy ○ Media Literacy ○ Information, Communications, and Technology Literacy	☐ Flexibility and Adaptability ☐ Initiative and Self-Direction ☐ Social and Cross-Cultural Skills ☐ Productivity and Accountability ☐ Leadership and Responsibility

In this tool, students synthesize information from a variety of sources and formulate a persuasive argument.

HOW TO USE THIS TOOL

1. Provide students with a topic and position statement or have students select their own.
2. Identify the audience to whom the students will be addressing their persuasive argument. The audience can be designated by the teacher, by small groups, or by the class as a whole. The audience can be simulated or real.
3. Provide students with examples of the three types of evidence—statistics, quotes, and examples—listed in the graphic organizer. Engage students in a discussion about how each of these types of evidence is effective in persuading others to think or act a certain way.
4. Students use a variety of resources to locate examples of each type of evidence that supports their position statement. You can supply these resources or students can conduct their own searches.
5. Using the evidence they have gathered, students prepare a persuasive argument to share with the class. You can dictate the format of the argument or allow students to develop the argument in a format of their choice.

TIPS FOR USING THIS TOOL

• If students select their own topic and position statement, you may need to spend some class time modeling how to develop a position statement.

• Be sure that the position statement clearly reflects one side of an argument and that the position statement would lead to a two-sided discussion of the topic. The position statement should clearly state the desired action or thinking.

- You can direct students to include a specific amount of evidence for each category.
- If students will be using web-based sources for evidence, you might include a discussion of how to judge the reliability and credibility of an Internet source (see "Picking the Right Site" on page 127).
- The more choices students have in choosing a topic, a position statement, sources of evidence, or a presentation format, the greater sense of ownership students will have in the activity.
- Students could work in small groups for this activity.
- Consider having students share their final persuasive arguments with a real audience. For example, if it is a written argument, they might submit it to the editorial section of a newspaper. If it is a presentation, students might speak to the school board, the local city council, or some other appropriate group for the topic.

USING TECHNOLOGY

- Ask students to brainstorm appropriate key words and phrases to use in an Internet search for evidence.
- Share a well-written blog with students that demonstrates how others use evidence to promote their points of view.
- Create a blog post about the topic and have students use it to share the evidence they have collected. Other students can react to the evidence through comments. At the end, have students read through all the blog comments and reflect on how effectively they persuaded others.

THINKING IT THROUGH

You can address these questions during class discussion, in small groups, in student journals, or in a variety of other ways.

- What criteria did you use to select your evidence? Were you successful in selecting the evidence that best fit your audience?
- When searching for evidence to support your position statement, what biases did you encounter? How did you separate fact from opinion?
- What could you have improved about the presentation of your persuasive argument?
- Why is it important to learn how to create a persuasive argument? What are some examples of how this skill might have been helpful in your everyday life?

Classroom Tools

Convince Me!

When presenting a persuasive argument, you need to make sure that you have strong evidence to support your position. Consider the three types of evidence below and list examples of each that you could use in presenting your case.

Topic: _____

My Position: _____

Audience: _____

Type of Evidence	Examples
Statistics Numbers or percentages. Be sure that these are factual by checking your sources carefully and cite your sources here.	
Quotes Direct quotes from leading authorities, popular celebrities, leaders, or experts. Consider your audience in choosing the quotes.	
Examples or Stories Examples and stories of your own or someone else's direct experience with the issue. Present the story or example in an interesting and compelling way.	

Use your evidence to create a persuasive argument for your position. Select a format for delivering your persuasive argument that you think will capture the attention of your audience.

Classroom Tools

Connect, Summarize, and Ask

Learning and Innovation Skills	Information, Media, and Technology Skills	Life and Career Skills (Check those to be addressed)
✓ Creativity and Innovation ✓ Critical Thinking and Problem Solving ✓ Communication ○ Collaboration	✓ Information Literacy ○ Media Literacy ○ Information, Communications, and Technology Literacy	☐ Flexibility and Adaptability ☐ Initiative and Self-Direction ☐ Social and Cross-Cultural Skills ☐ Productivity and Accountability ☐ Leadership and Responsibility

This tool can help students assess what they already know, make connections with new content, summarize the most important points, and narrow down questions they still have about the topic.

HOW TO USE THIS TOOL

1. In the "Connections" area, students include both information that is part of their prior knowledge about the topic and any new connections they have made with the new learning, such as noting similarities or differences.

2. In the "Summarize" area, students note what they think are important points to remember about the topic. Encourage students to think about why they have chosen certain information as "most important." Students should be prepared to explain their choices.

3. In the "Ask" area, students should write questions that either seek clarification of what they do not understand or seek additional information about the topic.

4. Use students' questions for a class discussion or as a basis for additional investigation.

TIPS FOR USING THIS TOOL

• Students can work in small groups to discuss answers to the questions they have generated.

• Have students work in small groups to build consensus on the three most important points from their study. They should then prepare a presentation that shares their important learning with the rest of the class.

USING TECHNOLOGY

• Have students post their questions on a blog so that classmates can offer input. Students across several classrooms can comment on the blog posts.

Classroom Tools

• Consider partnering with another school that is studying the same topic and have students from both schools collaborate online to investigate and answer the questions.

THINKING IT THROUGH

You can address these questions during class discussion, in small groups, in student journals, or in a variety of other ways.

• What criteria did you use in determining the most important ideas? What made them important to you?

• Why might different people find different information important?

• Review your questions. How does asking questions help you focus on the topic? Is asking questions easier or harder than summarizing? Why?

• How does making connections with what you already know about a topic help you learn?

Connect, Summarize, and Ask

Think about what you are learning by identifying what is familiar (connect), determining what is most important to remember (summarize), and developing questions for further investigation (ask). Note these below.

1. Connect
What did you already know or how is the information similar to something you already knew?

2. Summarize
What is most important to remember about this topic?

3. Ask
What don't you understand or what would you like more information about?

Classroom Tools

Creating Good Questions

Learning and Innovation Skills	Information, Media, and Technology Skills	Life and Career Skills (Check those to be addressed)
✓ Creativity and Innovation ✓ Critical Thinking and Problem Solving ✓ Communication ✓ Collaboration	○ Information Literacy ○ Media Literacy ○ Information, Communications, and Technology Literacy	☐ Flexibility and Adaptability ☐ Initiative and Self-Direction ☐ Social and Cross-Cultural Skills ☐ Productivity and Accountability ☐ Leadership and Responsibility

This tool helps students practice creating questions about a topic of study. Then, by researching the answers to those questions, they better retain the knowledge.

HOW TO USE THIS TOOL

1. Conduct a class discussion about what constitutes a good question.
2. Model developing good questions by giving examples from a previously studied topic. In drafting the model questions, use the assessment verbs list on page 82.
3. Students work with a partner to generate good questions about the topic they are studying. They record their questions in the left-hand column of the chart.
4. Students work together to answer the questions they have generated and enter their answers in the right-hand column. If students are locating their own resources to answer the questions, they should note the sources of the information in the answer column or off to the side.
5. Students reflect on and share how generating and answering questions helped them remember what they learned.

TIPS FOR USING THIS TOOL

• Have pairs of students exchange their questions. Each pair then answers the questions of the other pair.
• Provide both exemplars and nonexamplars of questions to help students learn how to craft quality questions.
• Have students write the questions they generate on note cards and randomly draw questions from the stack. First ask students to assess the quality of the question, then conduct a class discussion to answer the question. You can also break the class into small groups to process the questions.

Classroom Tools

• Use some of the best questions as part of the summative assessment on the topic. When students see their own questions used in this way, it builds interest in and students' ownership of the learning.

USING TECHNOLOGY

• Post the questions that students generate on a blog and ask students to respond to them as part of a blog comment. Students could also author their own blog, with other students commenting on one another's blogs.
• You can use the questions as a foundation for a wiki on the topic.
• Create a common list of questions using an online collaboration tool.
• Type the questions into an Internet search engine and share the results with the class. Then reframe the questions to see if there are different search results. Discuss the difference between the results and how the different wording of questions affected the search results. Encourage students to experiment with various key words and questions when conducting an Internet search for information.

THINKING IT THROUGH

You can address these questions during class discussion, in small groups, in student journals, or in a variety of other ways.

• How does creating good questions help you learn about the topic?
• Which question verbs were easiest to use? Which were the most difficult? Why?
• What criteria did you use to judge the quality of the questions? Reflect on your own questions. How well did you meet those criteria?

 81

Classroom Tools

Creating Good Questions

Review what you have learned about the topic by creating some high-quality questions using a variety of the verbs below. Write your questions in the left-hand column of the chart on the next page.

Then work with a partner to share your questions and, to review the content, together answer each question. Use the right-hand column to record the answers that you and your partner develop for each question.

ASSESSMENT VERBS

- ☐ Analyze
- ☐ Assess
- ☐ Categorize
- ☐ Choose
- ☐ Classify or group
- ☐ Combine
- ☐ Compare
- ☐ Compose
- ☐ Construct support for
- ☐ Contrast
- ☐ Create
- ☐ Critique
- ☐ Criticize
- ☐ Defend
- ☐ Define
- ☐ Describe
- ☐ Devise
- ☐ Evaluate
- ☐ Examine
- ☐ Explain
- ☐ Expand
- ☐ Formulate a theory
- ☐ Guess
- ☐ Identify
- ☐ Imagine
- ☐ Infer
- ☐ Interpret
- ☐ Interview
- ☐ Invent
- ☐ Justify
- ☐ Link
- ☐ List

- ☐ Modify
- ☐ Negotiate
- ☐ Outline
- ☐ Paraphrase
- ☐ Predict
- ☐ Put together
- ☐ Question
- ☐ Rank
- ☐ Recommend
- ☐ Retell
- ☐ Review
- ☐ Revise
- ☐ Show
- ☐ Simplify
- ☐ Summarize
- ☐ Support
- ☐ Suppose
- ☐ Theorize
- ☐ Write

Other Verbs:

- ☐ _____
- ☐ _____
- ☐ _____
- ☐ _____
- ☐ _____

Classroom Tools

My Questions	Our Answers

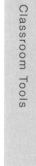

REFLECTION

How did creating and answering questions help you understand and remember what you learned?

 # Decision Tree

Learning and Innovation Skills	Information, Media, and Technology Skills	Life and Career Skills (Check those to be addressed)
✓ Creativity and Innovation ✓ Critical Thinking and Problem Solving ✓ Communication ✓ Collaboration	✓ Information Literacy ○ Media Literacy ○ Information, Communications, and Technology Literacy	☐ Flexibility and Adaptability ☐ Initiative and Self-Direction ☐ Social and Cross-Cultural Skills ☐ Productivity and Accountability ☐ Leadership and Responsibility

This tool guides students through brainstorming potential solutions to a problem, analyzing the options, and selecting and justifying which one is the best.

HOW TO USE THIS TOOL

1. Either identify a problem or ask students to identify a problem related to the topic they are studying. Be sure that the problem is stated clearly and that all students understand it.

2. Working alone or in small groups, students identify three potential solutions to the problem and enter them in the middle columns under the problem statement. If desired, all students can use a common set of three solutions.

3. Working individually, in pairs, or in small groups, students analyze the potential solutions by listing the pros and the cons of each and enter them into the appropriate blocks on each side of the potential solutions.

4. Students individually select the solution that they feel is best, and they explain the reasoning for their selection.

TIPS FOR USING THIS TOOL

• To determine the best solutions, students must understand the problem clearly. Take time to frame the problem and the situation that caused it.

• Help students understand that all solutions have both positives and negatives. The key is to find the solutions that will have the least negative effect and the greatest positive effect. Ask students to find examples of this from their own lives or from current events.

• Give students criteria to use in developing potential solutions. Is it cost-effective? Possible? Supported? Select criteria that match the problem.

• As a follow-up activity, students who selected the same solution can work together to create a media campaign to promote their solution.

USING TECHNOLOGY

• Once the problem has been framed, students can do an Internet search to locate ideas for solutions.

• Have students create a 30–60 second TV commercial promoting the solution they have chosen. If the whole class selected the solution, have students develop their commercial in small groups and then conduct a competition to select the best one.

• Ask students to create a brief summary of their solution, and then use on an online survey to have students vote for the best solution.

THINKING IT THROUGH

You can address these questions during class discussion, in small groups, in student journals, or in a variety of other ways.

• How did understanding the problem help you develop and analyze potential solutions?

• Why is it important to consider both the positives and negatives of a potential solution? Give an example from your own life.

• What criteria are most important in determining the solution to a problem? What factors would you take into account?

• If you worked with a group in this activity, how well did you communicate your thoughts to others in the group? How well did you listen to others' ideas? What did you do well? What could you improve?

Classroom Tools

  85

Decision Tree

When making a decision, it's important to consider all of your alternatives and the pros and cons for each potential solution.

1. Identify the problem you are trying to solve and write it in the top block.
2. Brainstorm three potential solutions to the problem, and write them in the center column.
3. List the positives about each solution in the left-hand column and the negatives in the right-hand column.
4. Choose a solution and summarize it at the end.

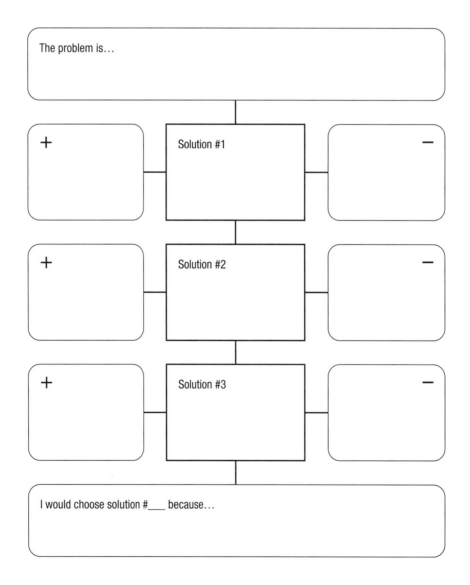

Developing Consensus

Learning and Innovation Skills	Information, Media, and Technology Skills	Life and Career Skills (Check to be addressed)
✓ Creativity and Innovation ✓ Critical Thinking and Problem Solving ✓ Communication ✓ Collaboration	○ Information Literacy ○ Media Literacy ○ Information, Communications, and Technology Literacy	☐ Flexibility and Adaptability ☐ Initiative and Self-Direction ☐ Social and Cross-Cultural Skills ☐ Productivity and Accountability ☐ Leadership and Responsibility

In this tool, the teacher introduces students to the concept of a consensus, and students practice negotiating, persuading, and compromising to reach a consensus about a decision or solution to a problem. You can use the tool with a whole class or small groups of students.

HOW TO USE THIS TOOL

1. Explain what *consensus* means:

   • Consensus does not necessarily mean total agreement; it means that all members of the group agree to implement the decision and not sabotage it. Some members of the group may have reservations about the decision, but if the group is in consensus, everyone will still work to support it.

   • Consensus is not established by a majority vote. Instead, it involves negotiating the decision or solution until everyone can agree to support it.

2. Clearly state the decision or solution about which the class or group is working toward consensus.

3. Ask students if they have any questions they need answered before starting the process of building a consensus. If students raise questions, spend some time responding to them in a group discussion.

4. When there are no more questions, seek consensus by asking students to show their level of support on a scale of 1–5:

   • 1 = I cannot support the solution or decision, and I will sabotage it.

   • 3 = I have reservations but will passively support the solution or decision.

   • 5 = I support the solution or decision and will actively support it.

   At the time of the vote, all members simultaneously show the number of fingers that represents their vote.

Classroom Tools

5. If all members of the group do not show a level of support of 3 or above,

    • Ask those voting lower what would need to change about the decision for them to vote at least 3.

    • Further group discussion is held, and students make changes to the decision or solution based on this discussion.

    • Students vote again on the revised decision or solution.

6. Once students have reached a consensus, the group can move toward developing an implementation plan for the decision or solution.

TIPS FOR USING THIS TOOL

• Stress that coming to consensus is not about majority rule, but rather about how to come to a decision that everyone agrees to support.

• If you use this tool prior to instruction, it can help build curiosity about the topic. Students can then compare their discussion with new information as it is presented and have a post-instructional group discussion that focuses on their prior misconceptions and strengthens their knowledge base.

• If you use the tool to help a group choose from among several options, you might also ask the group to create supporting rationale for their final choice.

USING TECHNOLOGY

• Consider using an online survey, such as SurveyMonkey, to gather consensus ratings and comments. Students can develop the survey and ask all class members to participate. Then the group can process the survey results to help refine their decision or solution.

• Each group can create a blog post about their potential decision or solutions. Students from within the class, across classes, or within a whole school can provide input and ideas for shaping the solution or decision.

THINKING IT THROUGH

You can address these questions during class discussion, in small groups, in student journals, or in a variety of other ways.

• Reflect on the consensus-building process and your role as a participant in it. Did you clearly state your opinions or viewpoint? Were you a blocker or facilitator of the process? How did you handle conflict?

- Describe how consensus-building is different than voting. Describe some situations in which consensus-building would be a better option than voting and explain why.
- How well did members of the group listen to one another? What did the group do to ensure that all members had a voice in the process?
- What would or could you personally have done differently to help build consensus?

Developing Consensus

Enter the decision or solution that you will be discussing. Indicate your level of agreement by showing 1–5 fingers.

> 1 = I cannot support and will sabotage the solution or decision.
>
> 3 = I have reservations about the solution or decision but will passively support it.
>
> 5 = I am in total agreement with the solution or decision and will actively support it.

Evaluate if there is enough consensus (the lowest score is a 3) to move forward. If not, discuss what it would take to reach a consensus and rewrite the decision or solution. Repeat this process until you reach a consensus.

DECISION OR SOLUTION:

Level of Consensus					
Group Member	1	2	3	4	5

ROUND 2 REVISED DECISION OR SOLUTION:

Level of Consensus					
Group Member	1	2	3	4	5

ROUND 3 REVISED DECISION OR SOLUTION:

Level of Consensus					
Group Member	1	2	3	4	5

Classroom Tools

Evaluating My Own Understanding

Learning and Innovation Skills	Information, Media, and Technology Skills	Life and Career Skills (Check those to be addressed)
○ Creativity and Innovation ✓ Critical Thinking and Problem Solving ○ Communication ○ Collaboration	✓ Information Literacy ○ Media Literacy ○ Information, Communications, and Technology Literacy	☐ Flexibility and Adaptability ☐ Initiative and Self-Direction ☐ Social and Cross-Cultural Skills ☐ Productivity and Accountability ☐ Leadership and Responsibility

This tool provides students with a form for reflecting on their understanding of information they've accessed on the Internet, read in a document, viewed in a video, or heard in a presentation.

HOW TO USE THIS TOOL

1. In answering the question, "What do I understand?" students summarize what they have learned, focusing specifically on new information or new connections they have made.

2. In answering the question, "What don't I understand?" students share questions they still have that require clarification or more information to increase their understanding.

3. In answering the question, "What additional information would I like to have?" students extend their learning by framing questions that go beyond the presented information.

4. Students rate their overall understanding of the information on a scale of 1–10:

   - 1 = I do not understand at all.
   - 5 = I have a lot of questions.
   - 10 = I understand it thoroughly.

   A rating of 10 does not mean that students do not have extension questions precipitated by their review of the information.

5. Use the clarification and extension questions that students generate as discussion points for small groups or the whole class.

TIPS FOR USING THIS TOOL

- Model the use of this tool by completing it as a whole class with some new content, or consider modeling with a topic that you have recently taught.

Classroom Tools

- Students may have difficulty separating clarification questions from extension questions. Encourage them to ask rich, thought-provoking questions rather than questions that are factual in nature.
- You can use the tool as a pre-instructional technique for encouraging students to access prior knowledge and think beyond the text or information.
- You can follow up the tool with a discussion about the value of reflecting on what you have learned and thinking about how well you understand what you have learned.

USING TECHNOLOGY

- Have students enter their clarification or extension questions into an online document. Then ask individuals or pairs of students to respond to the questions online. Review all responses as a class and discuss the answers. Note any discrepancies in answers and discuss how to validate the correct answer.
- Use an extension question as the basis for the development of a WebQuest or wikispace. Students can design their own WebQuest or wikispace, or you can consider designing one that all students will use to extend their understanding of the topic.
- Create a message board or use an online program, such as Stixy or Wallwisher, to share potential questions that students have framed.
- E-mail a question to all students and ask them to "reply to all" when they answer it. Different groups can process and collect ideas for answers to different questions, but all class members can see the responses.
- Have groups of students create a presentation that shares the answers they have formulated to a question that was generated by another student, the group, or the class.

THINKING IT THROUGH

You can address these questions during class discussion, in small groups, in student journals, or in a variety of other ways.

- What is different about identifying new information or ideas from summarizing the information? Why might it be important to identify new information or insights?
- Describe the thinking process you used to determine whether something was a new information or insight into the topic.
- How did you know when you truly did not understand something? How does asking a question help?
- How does asking questions about content that is not included help you learn about the topic? Did you ask meaningful questions that will result in a deeper understanding?

- Explain how you determined your own level of knowledge about the topic at the end of the activity. Why did you rate it as you did? What might help you increase your understanding?

Evaluating My Own Understanding

Reflecting on what you learn helps you think more deeply about the topic and helps you make connections between existing knowledge and the new information. After you have done some reading, watched a video, or listened to a presentation on the new topic, think about and answer the questions below.

Topic: _____

1. What do I understand about the topic now? What is the new information that I know now that I didn't know before?

2. What don't I understand yet? What do I need clarified?

3. What additional information would I like to have? What questions do I still have about the topic that was not part of the information?

4. On a scale of 1–10, my level of understanding about this topic is (circle one)

    1 = I do not understand at all.
    5 = I have a lot of questions.
    10 = I understand it thoroughly.

    1   2   3   4   5   6   7   8   9   10

Four Corners

Learning and Innovation Skills	Information, Media, and Technology Skills	Life and Career Skills (Check those to be addressed)
○ Creativity and Innovation ✓ Critical Thinking and Problem Solving ✓ Communication ✓ Collaboration	○ Information Literacy ○ Media Literacy ○ Information, Communications, and Technology Literacy	☐ Flexibility and Adaptability ☐ Initiative and Self-Direction ☐ Social and Cross-Cultural Skills ☐ Productivity and Accountability ☐ Leadership and Responsibility

This tool can help students think critically about information and develop and defend opinions based on facts.

HOW TO USE THIS TOOL

1. Either provide students with a controversial opinion statement about the topic being studied or ask students to develop one collaboratively. The controversy should be phrased in a way that engenders a wide range of viewpionts.

2. Students determine whether they strongly agree, agree, disagree, or strongly disagree with the statement.

3. Students individually list the reasons for their opinions.

4. Designate each of the room's four corners as representing "strongly agree," "agree," "disagree," or "strongly disagree."

5. Signal students when it is time for them to move to the corner of the room that corresponds to their opinion. All students move at the same time, bringing their lists with them.

6. Each group compares their list of reasons and establishes the three most compelling supports for their position on the statement.

7. Begin with the "strongly agree" corner and have a spokesperson for the group report on the group's consensus on reasons they strongly agree with the statement. Each corner reports in turn without any discussion or debate.

8. After all groups have reported, students return to their seats.

9. Conduct additional instruction or investigation on the topic.

10. Repeat the process of students determining their level of agreement, listing individual reasons, and then coming to an agreement with others on the three most important reasons for their position (steps 2–6).

11. Assign a follow-up activity, such as a debate, persuasive essay, or presentation, if desired, in which students defend their opinions.

TIPS FOR USING THIS TOOL

• Requiring students to mark down their level of agreement and then all move at the same time eliminates the chance that students will be influenced by their friends.

• Stress that it is acceptable for students to change their positions once they have learned more about the topic. The goal is for students to think critically about the information and not become set on an opinion.

• If there is not a great diversity of opinion among students on the topic, you can randomly assign students to defend a position.

• Emphasize the importance of students actively listening to other groups. You can ask students to summarize the new information they gleaned from other groups.

USING TECHNOLOGY

• Using Google Docs, or some other collaborative editing tool, students can collectively add ideas to support their position.

• Have students enter the reasons for their opinions onto a PowerPoint slide and share their work with others. You can also use the slides to help students prepare for a follow-up project.

THINKING IT THROUGH

You can address these questions during class discussion, in small groups, in student journals, or in a variety of other ways.

• Why do people often have diverse opinions on the same topic? What influences your opinions?

• Describe the process you used to think about the topic and determine why you believe what you do.

• Were you an active listener when others were reporting out? What evidence do you have that you were a good listener? How can you improve your listening skills?

Classroom Tools

Four Corners

1. Determine your level of agreement with the following statement:

   _____

   _____

☐ Strongly Agree	☐ Agree	☐ Disagree	☐ Strongly Disagree

2. List your reasons for your level of agreement below.

3. Take your paper and move to the corner of the room designated with your level of agreement. Then share your reasons for your opinion with the group.

4. As a group, choose the three best reasons for your level of agreement. Be prepared to share your reasons with the rest of the class.

OUR REASONS

1. _____

   _____

2. _____

   _____

3. _____

   _____

Four Corners

5. After investigating the topic further, what is your level of agreement with the original statement?

☐ Strongly Agree	☐ Agree	☐ Disagree	☐ Strongly Disagree

6. What additional information did you gather that affected your level of agreement? What new information did you gain from your investigation? Note the new information below.

Classroom Tools

Framing the Problem

Learning and Innovation Skills	Information, Media, and Technology Skills	Life and Career Skills (Check those to be addressed)
○ Creativity and Innovation ✓ Critical Thinking and Problem Solving ○ Communication ○ Collaboration	✓ Information Literacy ○ Media Literacy ○ Information, Communications, and Technology Literacy	☐ Flexibility and Adaptability ☐ Initiative and Self-Direction ☐ Social and Cross-Cultural Skills ☐ Productivity and Accountability ☐ Leadership and Responsibility

This tool is designed to help students understand a problem by providing them with a format to organize statistics, opinions, emotions, and the potential effect of a problem. By researching these characteristics, students can better understand a problem and develop informed solutions.

HOW TO USE THIS TOOL

1. Identify a problem area that relates to the topic being studied.
2. Discuss each category of information for a problem—statistics, opinions, emotions, and effect—and define the characteristics of each before students begin the activity.
3. Students research the topic to identify the statistics, opinions, and emotions connected to it and the potential effect of the topic. Students can also include the inferences (see "Processing the Data" on page 142) they make from the information or add personal observations. However, they should include at least some information from other sources.
4. Students review the information in each box and develop a problem statement that clearly defines the issue or problem.
5. Once you have approved the problem statement, students can conduct further research or study based on the defined problem.

TIPS FOR USING THIS TOOL

• Discuss the difference between fact and opinion before starting the activity. Provide students with examples from everyday life.
• Discuss the role of emotions in understanding and solving problems.
• Students could work in small groups to complete the activity.
• All students can work on the same topic or problem, or students can choose an area related to the current topic of study.

- Consider having students cite the sources of their information.
- Consider assigning students a specific perspective or viewpoint to use in completing the activity. Different sections of the class might be assigned different perspectives. Share and discuss how a person's viewpoint might have affected the information cited in each category. (Note: "The Viewpoint" on page 178 can help students develop different perspectives on the topic.)
- Have students use the information from the completed graphic organizer to develop a presentation that will compel others to become interested in the problem. The activity can also be a springboard for developing a persuasive argument.
- The resulting problem statement can serve as the foundation for a project-based learning activity or a student-led inquiry.

USING TECHNOLOGY

- Consider using an online collaboration tool to compile student input into each category.
- Have students use a social bookmarking tool to compile a list of online resources that students used to research the problem.
- Have students conduct an online survey of their peers, parents, or others to provide input about the problem, especially in the areas of opinions and emotions.
- Create a blog post that solicits input to the problem to gather ideas.
- Create a wiki on the problem area to share resources and information sources.

THINKING IT THROUGH

You can address these questions during class discussion, in small groups, in student journals, or in a variety of other ways.

- Why is it important to clearly understand a problem before attempting to solve it?
- How might emotions influence someone's view of a problem or situation? Give an example of when your own emotions affected your opinions about a situation.
- How important are statistics in understanding a problem? What must you be careful about in using statistics to frame a problem?
- Which of the four types of information was most difficult for you to identify? What made it more difficult than the others?
- How well do you think your problem statement reflects the root causes of the problem?

Classroom Tools

Framing the Problem

Before you can develop sound solutions, you must first understand the problem that you are trying to solve. Identify statistics, opinions, emotions, and effects of a problem by entering notes on each in the appropriate box. Then develop a problem statement in the middle that you believe addresses the real problem.

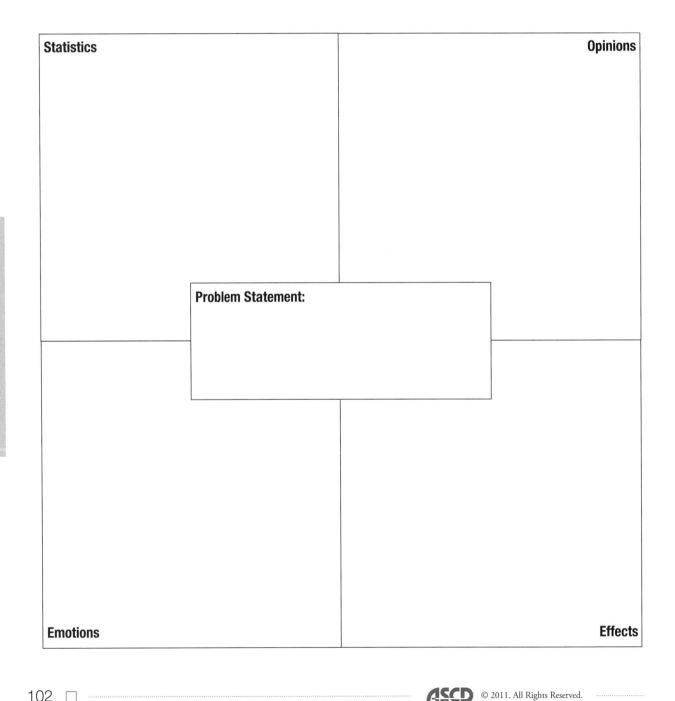

Ground Rules for Teams

Learning and Innovation Skills	Information, Media, and Technology Skills	Life and Career Skills (Check those to be addressed)
○ Creativity and Innovation ○ Critical Thinking and Problem Solving ✓ Communication ✓ Collaboration	○ Information Literacy ○ Media Literacy ○ Information, Communications, and Technology Literacy	☐ Flexibility and Adaptability ☐ Initiative and Self-Direction ☐ Social and Cross-Cultural Skills ☐ Productivity and Accountability ☐ Leadership and Responsibility

At the beginning of the year or when new teams or groups are formed, this tool can help the class establish rules of conduct for working together.

HOW TO USE THIS TOOL

1. Share with students the purpose for ground rules and how they will govern team work. The rules guide interactions within the group and establish boundaries for group processes.

2. Using input from all of members of the group, students collect suggestions for rules of conduct for the group during team sessions. Consider having students state the ground rules in a positive way (what to do) instead of a negative way (what not to do). For example, instead of, "No side conversations," the rule might be phrased as, "Give full attention to the person speaking."

3. After you have gathered all of the suggestions, establish a consensus (see "Developing Consensus" on page 87) around the rules the class will adopt. Remember that consensus does not necessarily mean total agreement, but members should agree to abide by the rules.

4. Post the rules so that they are visible to all members during meetings. One group member can be appointed to ensure that the rules are followed, although any member can point out infractions at any time. The group leader has the final power to enforce any of the rules.

TIPS FOR USING THIS TOOL

• If this is the first time students have been exposed to the concept of ground rules, it may be helpful to provide some suggested rules, such as, "Only one person speaks at a time" and "Actively listen to one another."

Classroom Tools

ASCD ☐ 103

- To help provide an orderly environment for the exchange of ideas in the classroom, you can establish ground rules for the entire class and post them at the front of the room.
- If the same groups meet frequently, consider printing the team's ground rules on a table tent that is visible to all group members at all times. If the group uses an agenda for their work, the ground rules can also be printed at the top of each meeting agenda.
- If groups are having trouble with members not following their rules, you should intervene by reviewing the rules, reestablishing consensus, and stepping in when necessary to help enforce them.

USING TECHNOLOGY

- Ask students to prepare a 30-second commercial that demonstrates the importance of one of the ground rules.
- Find video clips that demonstrate what happens when members of a team do not follow the rules.
- Have students design an online survey about the ground rules before they are adopted. The survey could include students from across classes and seek input about the level of agreement. In addition, an open-ended question could ask participants to provide examples of how the ground rule might help the group be productive or to suggest ways to improve the rule.

THINKING IT THROUGH

You can address these questions during class discussion, in small groups, in student journals, or in a variety of other ways.

- Every group behaves based on a common code of what is acceptable. Sometimes this code of conduct is not written down, but everyone knows what the rules are. Give an example of an unwritten code of conduct that exists for a group you belong to.
- Why are ground rules important for teams that are trying to work together?
- If a group member is not abiding by the ground rules, what can team members do? What do you think should happen if a team member continues to violate the rules? Who is responsible for enforcing the ground rules?
- Evaluate your own behavior in obeying the ground rules of the team. What was the most difficult rule to follow? Why? How did you change, or could you have changed, your behavior to follow the rule?
- Why is it important for teams to establish a consensus about the ground rules? Did your group do a good job of getting everyone to agree? Why or why not?

Ground Rules for Teams

Once your team has established and adopted its ground rules, it is the responsibility of every team member to follow them.

1. Enter your adopted ground rules in the first column of the chart below.
2. At the end of the group meeting, reflect on how well you abided by the ground rules by ranking your level of compliance.

    1 = Not at all

    5 = Completely

3. Write a brief statement about how you can improve your team skills.

Ground Rules	My Level of Compliance (1–5)

IMPROVING MY SKILLS

Based on your participation in today's group work, how could you improve your team skills?

I'm Sure of It...or Not

Learning and Innovation Skills	Information, Media, and Technology Skills	Life and Career Skills (Check those to be addressed)
○ Creativity and Innovation ✓ Critical Thinking and Problem Solving ✓ Communication ○ Collaboration	○ Information Literacy ○ Media Literacy ○ Information, Communications, and Technology Literacy	☐ Flexibility and Adaptability ☐ Initiative and Self-Direction ☐ Social and Cross-Cultural Skills ☐ Productivity and Accountability ☐ Leadership and Responsibility

This tool can help students recall what they already know about an area of study you are about to introduce. The tool also asks students to assess how certain they are about the accuracy of their prior knowledge.

HOW TO USE THIS TOOL

1. Prior to instruction, ask students to recall everything they know—or think they know—about the topic and have them record their thoughts in the first column of the organizer.

2. Students should also indicate how sure they are about the information they are sharing by categorizing their prior knowledge as

   - 90–100% sure
   - 50–89% sure
   - Less than 50% sure

3. Assure students that everyone has incorrect information and provide examples of this. (Even scientists at one time said there were nine planets!)

4. After they have entered all of their thoughts, students write a brief explanation about why they chose the level of surety that they did.

5. As students learn more about the topic, they revisit their list to confirm correct understandings and correct misconceptions.

TIPS FOR USING THIS TOOL

• Start instruction as soon as possible after the activity. If possible, have students review their prior knowledge and begin instruction within the same class period.

• Students can work in pairs or small groups to list what they know or think they know. This is especially helpful if most students do not have extensive background knowledge about the topic.

- Help students feel comfortable in identifying misinformation. The purpose of the activity is to help students examine their own thinking and knowledge base.
- As students learn more about the topic, have them star or highlight the facts and ideas that were correct. They can also correct any incorrect preconceptions about the topic.
- You can conduct the activity as a whole class and make public notes of contributions. Be sure to allow some individual time, however, for students to process their thinking before sharing with the class.

USING TECHNOLOGY

- Have students use Internet sources to find supporting documentation for the facts about which they were "90–100% sure." Students can also use the Internet to locate information that clarifies facts about which they are not certain.

THINKING IT THROUGH

You can address these questions during class discussion, in small groups, in student journals, or in a variety of other ways.

- Describe how you made decisions about your level of certainty about what you knew. What criteria did you use?
- What helped trigger your memories about the topic? How do you think you can use these triggers to help you learn in other areas?
- Why is it important to think about what you know prior to learning something new?

I'm Sure of It...or Not

Think about what you already know about the topic that you will be studying. Enter each item into the appropriate category, based on how sure you are about the fact. Explain why you are sure—or not!—in the right-hand column.

What I Know or Think I Know About _____

I'm 90–100% sure that...	Because...
I'm 50–89% sure that...	Because...
I'm less than 50% sure that...	Because...

Investigation by Three

Learning and Innovation Skills	Information, Media, and Technology Skills	Life and Career Skills (Check those to be addressed)
○ Creativity and Innovation ✓ Critical Thinking and Problem Solving ✓ Communication ✓ Collaboration	✓ Information Literacy ○ Media Literacy ✓ Information, Communications, and Technology Literacy	☐ Flexibility and Adaptability ☐ Initiative and Self-Direction ☐ Social and Cross-Cultural Skills ☐ Productivity and Accountability ☐ Leadership and Responsibility

This tool guides students, working in groups, in formulating and researching questions they have about a topic of study. The tool can help introduce a new topic or be used to extend knowledge.

HOW TO USE THIS TOOL

1. Break the class into groups of three.
2. Each group develops three questions about the major ideas or concepts of an assigned topic.
3. Groups discuss what they already know that might answer each of their questions.
4. All members of the groups research the questions individually, using resources of their choice or that you have assigned. Encourage students to use at least one online source to locate information.
5. Students share within their groups the information they have found that answers each question, and they record the information shared by others on their own sheets.
6. Either individually or as a group, students develop a summary sentence that answers each question.

TIPS FOR USING THIS TOOL

- Students can select their own groups or you can assign them randomly.
- Encourage students to dig deeply into their knowledge to share what they think they already know about the answer to the question. Allow them to air their misconceptions by assuring them that wrong answers at this point are OK.
- Suggest that students take brief notes about their research, emphasizing the use of key words or phrases.

Classroom Tools

• Discuss what groups could do if they have found discrepancies in the information that answers a question. Do they need to do more research? How can they verify the correct information?

• Provide time limits or guidelines for each step of the activity. Remind students when time is up for each component, and give a one-minute warning before the end of each step.

USING TECHNOLOGY

• Compile all of the summary sentences into a master list in a PowerPoint slide, word processing document, or some other program that will allow you to project the answers for the whole class to review.

• Project a timer that counts down the remaining time for each phase of the activity so that students can monitor their progress.

THINKING IT THROUGH

You can address these questions during class discussion, in small groups, in student journals, or in a variety of other ways.

• How did thinking about what you already knew about the topic help guide your search for answers?

• Were your questions meaty enough to be worth researching?

• How did you handle conflicting information? What process did you use to confirm or eliminate answers?

• Why is it important to use information from more than one source to answer a question? Give examples of when this might be important in your daily life.

Investigation by Three

Working in groups of three, develop questions about the topic. Your questions should require you to think deeply about the topic.

1. Write the topic and questions in the top row of the chart below.
2. As a group, discuss what you already know about each question and briefly record your responses in the second row.
3. Individually investigate each question using any resources you wish.
4. After completing your research, share your information with the group and write a summary sentence that answers each question.

Topic:	Question 1:	Question 2:	Question 3:
What we already know about the question			
Information gathered by group member #1			
Information gathered by group member #2			
Information gathered by group member #3			
Summary sentence that answers the question.			

Classroom Tools

 111

Learn, Discuss, and Summarize

Learning and Innovation Skills	Information, Media, and Technology Skills	Life and Career Skills (Check those to be addressed)
○ Creativity and Innovation ✓ Critical Thinking and Problem Solving ✓ Communication ✓ Collaboration	✓ Information Literacy ○ Media Literacy ○ Information, Communications, and Technology Literacy	☐ Flexibility and Adaptability ☐ Initiative and Self-Direction ☐ Social and Cross-Cultural Skills ☐ Productivity and Accountability ☐ Leadership and Responsibility

In this tool, students record, discuss, and summarize their new learning about a topic of study. Students practice identifying big ideas and key information and making connections with their existing knowledge.

HOW TO USE THIS TOOL

1. Conduct a class discussion about distinguishing new information from information that students already know.

2. Model the tool with a piece of text or video on a topic already familiar to students, asking students to identify either new information or new insights or connections they can make as they read the text or watch the video.

3. Students list the new information they learned or new connections they made from the lesson. They note these in the top row.

4. As a whole group or in small groups, students share what they have learned. Then students list any additional new learning or connections about the topic in the middle row.

5. Students summarize their new learning from both the presentation and the discussion. Their summary statements should reflect what they believe is the most important information they gleaned from both.

TIPS FOR USING THIS TOOL

• Encourage students to include both new facts and new connections they have made about the content.

• Small groups can process the information together, using public notes on chart paper.

• Help students understand the importance of making connections between what they already know and what they are learning. These connections help them retain the information for future use.

- Students can work in pairs to summarize the key ideas.
- Reinforce the importance of listening with focus to deepen understanding.

USING TECHNOLOGY

- You could allow students to find one of their own sources of information. If the sources of information are from the Internet, make sure that students check the dates and sources of the information to ensure that it is reliable and valid. (See "Picking the Right Site" on page 127.)
- Students can record their summary ideas on a Google Doc or build on previous information that's stored in a wiki.

THINKING IT THROUGH

You can address these questions during class discussion, in small groups, in student journals, or in a variety of other ways.

- Describe the way you process information in determining whether it is new or not.
- What's the value of revisiting or rethinking about information that you have already studied?
- Why might it be important to separate new information from what you already know?
- Do you think you learned more on your own or when you were working with others? Why?

Learn, Discuss, and Summarize

Topic: _____

Notes from the Text or Presentation: New Learning or Connections

Notes from Class Discussion: Additional New Learning or Connections

Summary: Based on what you have learned, what are the most important things to remember about the topic?

Making Good Decisions

Learning and Innovation Skills	Information, Media, and Technology Skills	Life and Career Skills (Check those to be addressed)
✓ Creativity and Innovation ✓ Critical Thinking and Problem Solving ✓ Communication ✓ Collaboration	○ Information Literacy ○ Media Literacy ○ Information, Communications, and Technology Literacy	☐ Flexibility and Adaptability ☐ Initiative and Self-Direction ☐ Social and Cross-Cultural Skills ☐ Productivity and Accountability ☐ Leadership and Responsibility

In this tool, students develop criteria for assessing the alternatives of a decision. They then apply their criteria to a decision related to the topic of study and share with the class the reasoning for their choice.

HOW TO USE THIS TOOL

1. Clearly define the decision that students are going to make that is related to the topic being studied.
2. Students brainstorm a list of criteria against which they can judge potential solutions or decisions. They list these criteria in the top of each column.
3. Students brainstorm solutions that could address the decision and record them in the "Alternatives" column.
4. Students assess each alternative against the criteria by rating it on a scale of 1–5:
   - 1 = Does not match the criteria.
   - 5 = Strongly and clearly meets the criteria.
5. Students total the scores of each alternative and write the total in the last column.
6. Students pick the alternative that they think is the best solution and prepare a justification for their choice.
7. In a class discussion, students share their choices and reasons for supporting them.

TIPS FOR USING THIS TOOL

- Help students understand the process by modeling it with an everyday decision before using it with subject-area content.
- Be sure to state the decision so that it lends itself to multiple alternatives.
- Consider involving students in developing the decision statement or question.

Classroom Tools

- Ensure that students have enough background information about the decision to be able to develop logical alternatives.
- Small groups of students can develop alternatives and criteria and then select the alternative they feel is best. Each group could then prepare a presentation and share their choice with the rest of the class. Once all groups have shared, the class as a whole can select an alternative and support it with rationale.
- If students judge that some criteria are more important than others, they can assign each criterion with a weight of 1 (less important) to 3 (most important). When calculating the score for each criterion, students would multiply the rating by the weight for each factor.

USING TECHNOLOGY

- To engage the whole class in the process, develop an online survey to which students would reply with their rankings of each criterion. The survey could also be completed by an audience from beyond the classroom. To gather details about respondents' rationale for their ratings, the survey could include an open-ended section.
- You can group students to conduct further investigation on the Internet about each alternative.
- Create a wiki for students to use in compiling information about various alternatives and to link to their presentations.
- In presenting their choices, students can use a variety of electronic tools.

THINKING IT THROUGH

You can address these questions during class discussion, in small groups, in student journals, or in a variety of other ways.

- Why is it important to think about many alternatives when making an important decision?
- How does defining the criteria for selecting an alternative help you make a better decision?
- Give an example of an important decision you had to make and how using an organized process of looking at criteria might have been helpful.
- Was it more difficult to think of alternatives or to develop the criteria? Why?

Making Good Decisions

When making an important decision, it is helpful to carefully weigh the alternatives before deciding on a course of action.

1. List the alternatives down the left side of the table below.
2. Think about the criteria that are important in making a decision and write them in the top row.
3. Rate each alternative against the criteria on a scale of 1–5:
    1 = Does not match the criteria.
    5 = Strongly and clearly meets the criteria.
4. Total the score of each alternative in the last column.

Decision to be made: _____

_____

Criteria →						Score
Alternative 1:						
Alternative 2:						
Alternative 3:						

Classroom Tools

Making Good Decisions

	Criteria ➜					Score
Alternative 4:						

YOUR ALTERNATIVE

Evaluate the score of each alternative, and select an alternative.

My alternative is:_____

JUSTIFICATION

Explain why you made the decision you did below. Be prepared to share your decision and your justification for it with the class.

My Action Plan

Learning and Innovation Skills	Information, Media, and Technology Skills	Life and Career Skills (Check those to be addressed)
○ Creativity and Innovation ✓ Critical Thinking and Problem Solving ✓ Communication ○ Collaboration	✓ Information Literacy ○ Media Literacy ✓ Information, Communications, and Technology Literacy	☐ Flexibility and Adaptability ☐ Initiative and Self-Direction ☐ Social and Cross-Cultural Skills ☐ Productivity and Accountability ☐ Leadership and Responsibility

In this tool, students practice creating a research plan to find information about a major idea or concept.

HOW TO USE THIS TOOL

1. Discuss how searching for answers or information is analogous to planning a trip: careful planning results in a more enjoyable experience!
2. Either provide students with a question that frames their investigation or assist them in creating their own questions. The question should require a depth of understanding about the topic or spur investigation.
3. Students record what they already know or think they know that might partially answer the big question.
4. Students identify the types of information they will collect to answer the big question and develop plans for how they will collect that information.
5. Students conduct and record their search.
6. As students locate information and after they have reviewed the information they found, they record new questions they have about the topic. These questions can provide the focus for ongoing investigation or the basis for class discussion.

TIPS FOR USING THIS TOOL

• Ensure that students' big question, which frames the investigation, is worthy of extended research. It should cause students to think deeply and widely about the topic, and students should have to assimilate a wide variety of information to answer it.

• It might be helpful to discuss the variety of sources, including print, online, and primary sources, that students could use to collect information about the question.

Classroom Tools

☐ 119

- Students can share the results of their research in small groups, comparing information and sharing their questions. One student in the group may have located information that answers another group member's questions. If there are any questions that the group cannot answer together, they can bring them to the whole class for discussion.

USING TECHNOLOGY

- Ask students to identify key words or phrases that they could use in conducting an Internet search to answer the question.
- Post the new questions students generate on a blog or online collaboration site, and have the class respond to the questions.
- Have students use social bookmarking tools to compile a list of useful websites, annotating each website with a brief description of what is included on the website.
- Create a wiki where students can access blogs about the big question, compile a list of websites, and upload summaries of the activity.

THINKING IT THROUGH

You can address these questions during class discussion, in small groups, in student journals, or in a variety of other ways.

- Explain the importance of having a high-quality big question that frames your investigation.
- Why is it helpful to think about what you already know or think you know about the question before you start to investigate it?
- Did you find that you had any misinformation or misconceptions about the topic before you started to research it? How did the new information change your mind?
- How does having a plan for your research help you become more effective in your search for answers? How could you use such a plan in other situations?

My Action Plan

Before you begin your quest for answers, plan your search by thinking about the steps below and making some notes that will guide your search.

The big question: _____

What I already know, or think I know, that might help answer the big question:	
Information I'll Collect	**How I'll Collect the Information**

AFTER COLLECTING THE INFORMATION

Once you have completed your search, summarize what you have learned and then list any new questions about the topic.

Summary of Information	New Questions

Our Shared Learning

Learning and Innovation Skills	Information, Media, and Technology Skills	Life and Career Skills (Check those to be addressed)
✓ Creativity and Innovation ✓ Critical Thinking and Problem Solving ✓ Communication ✓ Collaboration	○ Information Literacy ○ Media Literacy ○ Information, Communications, and Technology Literacy	☐ Flexibility and Adaptability ☐ Initiative and Self-Direction ☐ Social and Cross-Cultural Skills ☐ Productivity and Accountability ☐ Leadership and Responsibility

Students can use this tool to share with one another what they already know or have learned about a topic of study.

HOW TO USE THIS TOOL

1. Explain the three categories of information—key ideas, what they already knew, and examples or applications—students will seek from each other in the activity.
2. Ask students to prepare at least one answer for each category.
3. Have students move around the room asking other students to provide information for one of the three categories.
4. Students continue to share until everyone has filled in all nine spaces. No square should repeat information from another square.
5. As a class, students share some examples from the graphic organizer.

TIPS FOR USING THIS TOOL

• Model the activity with a topic or content that is familiar to students.
• Make sure students keep moving; don't allow them to spend too much time with one person. Consider using a timer and have students move at the end of each time period.
• Direct students to not debate answers from others during the sharing time. They'll have the opportunity to discuss any questions during the follow-up class discussion.
• As a follow-up activity, allow time for small groups to share the ideas they have gathered and to discuss any that they question, need to clarify, or want more information about.

USING TECHNOLOGY

• Complete the matrix using an online collaboration tool. Load the graphic into a web-based tool, such as Google Docs, and ask students to enter at least one idea for each category.

 ☐ 123

Classroom Tools

• Create a blog post for each category and have students respond to each with their own ideas or input.

THINKING IT THROUGH

You can address these questions during class discussion, in small groups, in student journals, or in a variety of other ways.

• Which category was the most difficult for others to share? Why do you think this was the case?

• Which category was most difficult for you? Why?

• How does reflecting on what you already know about a topic help you learn more?

• What criteria did you use to identify a key idea about the topic? Do you think others' key ideas met these criteria?

• How would you help others do a better job of determining key ideas?

Classroom Tools

Our Shared Learning

1. Note one key idea, one piece of information you already knew, and one example or application in the spaces below that you will share with your classmates.
2. Meet with other classmates and exchange insights and ideas about what you have learned thus far. Note below what your classmates have shared, with one response per box. You must complete all nine boxes.
3. Think about what you learned from your classmates. Circle the boxes that reflect this new knowledge.

WHAT I CAN SHARE

My key idea:_____

Information I already knew:_____

_____

Example or application:_____

FROM MY CLASSMATES

Key Ideas			

Classroom Tools

What They Already Knew		
Example or Application		

Picking the Right Site

Learning and Innovation Skills	Information, Media, and Technology Skills	Life and Career Skills (Check those to be addressed)
○ Creativity and Innovation ✓ Critical Thinking and Problem Solving ✓ Communication ✓ Collaboration	✓ Information Literacy ✓ Media Literacy ✓ Information, Communications, and Technology Literacy	☐ Flexibility and Adaptability ☐ Initiative and Self-Direction ☐ Social and Cross-Cultural Skills ☐ Productivity and Accountability ☐ Leadership and Responsibility

In this tool, students practice assessing the credibility of websites and scanning web pages for useful information so that they have the skills to effectively search the web.

HOW TO USE THIS TOOL

1. Model how to evaluate a website in terms of credibility and how well the site matches the purpose of the search. Discuss how to assess the credibility of a website:

    -   Who created it?
    -   Are they trying to persuade the visitor?
    -   How current is the information?

2. Either assign students a website to review or have them select one they believe is appropriate to the topic being studied.
3. Students scan through the website, noting key words, headings, pictures, and so forth to develop a series of questions that they think might be answered with the information on the site.
4. Students share their work in pairs or small groups.
5. Conduct a class discussion on the results of the previews, with students reflecting on how they assessed the credibility of the website and used the site's features to create questions.

TIPS FOR USING THIS TOOL

-   Make sure that the students understand exactly which aspects of a topic they are investigating, especially if they are choosing their own website to preview.
-   All students can review the same website or you can assign different students or groups to different websites. If all students use the same website, small groups can compare their reviews and answer the questions they have generated.

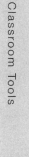

Classroom Tools

- If students are selecting their own websites, encourage them to abandon the site if their initial scan of it indicates that the information may be biased or not credible or if the site does not seem to cover the topic in a significant way.
- You can use the questions students generate for a continuing investigation on the topic, or students can use them as a basis for a continuing search for information.
- If students use different websites, they can exchange questions and websites with a partner. Each would then use the website to attempt to answer the questions that were generated for that site.

USING TECHNOLOGY

- As students scan the website to develop questions, have them note key words and terms that they could use in additional web searches.
- From the questions students generate, create a WebQuest for the same sites students used during the activity. Students can then work through the WebQuest as a way to enhance their understanding of the topic.

THINKING IT THROUGH

You can address these questions during class discussion, in small groups, in student journals, or in a variety of other ways.

- Describe your thinking as you searched the website for the key words and phrases that helped you frame your questions.
- What is important to remember about assessing the credibility of the source of a website?
- Why would taking time to scan or preview a website be important?
- How could developing questions from the preview help you use the website more efficiently? Where else could you apply this concept?

Picking the Right Site

When searching for specific information on the Internet, finding the right site is vital to being efficient in your search. To determine if the site fits your purpose,

1. Determine if the site is credible.
2. Scan the site to see if it has the information you need.

URL of website: _____

Author or sponsor: _____

Date of information: _____

1. Explain why you believe the website information is credible.

2. Scan through the website, noting key words and phrases, headings, pictures and graphics, and other clues that give you some ideas about what is included. Then develop several key questions that you think you would be able to answer from the information on the website.

   Question 1:

   Question 2:

   Question 3:

   Question 4:

   Question 5:

Classroom Tools

Planning My Learning

Learning and Innovation Skills	Information, Media, and Technology Skills	Life and Career Skills (Check those to be addressed)
✓ Creativity and Innovation ✓ Critical Thinking and Problem Solving ○ Communication ○ Collaboration	✓ Information Literacy ○ Media Literacy ✓ Information, Communications, and Technology Literacy	☐ Flexibility and Adaptability ☐ Initiative and Self-Direction ☐ Social and Cross-Cultural Skills ☐ Productivity and Accountability ☐ Leadership and Responsibility

This tool guides students through outlining the steps they will take to search for answers to questions they generated for a given topic. Then they follow through on their learning plan and reflect on the results of their inquiry.

HOW TO USE THIS TOOL

1. Introduce the topic that students will be investigating, being sure to provide enough information to engage their thinking.

2. Model the entire process of creating a learning plan, stressing the importance of creating good questions that lead to a deep understanding of the topic.

3. Students develop a list of questions that reflect the big questions that they will pursue as they investigate the topic.

4. Either provide students with a list of sources to use in answering their questions or have students brainstorm their own lists of potential sources.

5. Students create a learning plan, which is an outline of the steps they will take to search for answers.

6. Students search the sources, recording information that answers one or more of their questions. They indicate the source of the information and identify the question that the information either wholly or partially answers.

7. After completing their review of the sources, students evaluate their success in completing the inquiry by checking the responses included in the "Evaluating My Success" portion of the planner.

8. Students reflect on their results and develop questions that they might use in further investigations about the topic. You can use these questions as the basis for a class discussion to enhance students' understanding of the topic.

TIPS FOR USING THIS TOOL

• To help students think broadly about the topic and develop diverse questions, create a concept map of subtopics related to the subject.

• Consider having students work in groups to complete the inquiry. They would generate their questions together, brainstorm potential resources to use, and pool their responses.

• You can ask different groups of students to investigate different aspects of the topic. After completing the inquiry, students can present their findings to the rest of the class.

• Students can use the questions for further study as the foundation for a new learning plan.

• Conduct a discussion about the process of inquiry. Ask students to reflect on and describe how they could use this process whenever they are learning something new.

USING TECHNOLOGY

• Ask students to brainstorm a list of key words or phrases related to the topic that might help them locate resources.

• If they are using Google, have students conduct an advanced search using the Google Wonder Wheel tool.

• Encourage students to use a wide variety of sources, such as documents, visuals, presentations, or videos, in their search for answers.

• Use a collaborative writing tool, such as Google Docs, to have students compile their list of questions and answers.

• Use a social bookmarking site or a wiki and have students collectively contribute quality sources of information. They could also annotate each source to help guide others in using the most appropriate sources for their investigations.

THINKING IT THROUGH

You can address these questions during class discussion, in small groups, in student journals, or in a variety of other ways.

• What part of your learning plan was the most difficult to complete? What problems did you have carrying out your plan?

• How did having a plan for investigation help you?

• How did you determine what a good question would be about the topic?

• What advice would you give others who are using this format to guide their inquiry on a topic?

• How could you use this tool in another content area or with another topic?

Classroom Tools

Planning My Learning

Having a plan for learning will help you be more efficient and effective in achieving your learning goals. Use the questions below to plan your learning and record the findings of your research.

Name:_____

Topic:_____

MAKING THE PLAN

	What I Want to Know List questions you have about the topic.
1	
2	
3	
4	
5	

Potential Sources of Information Identify the sources of information that you think will be helpful in answering your questions.

Planning My Learning

	The Plan Describe the steps you will take to carry out your learning plan. Include as many steps as necessary to adequately describe how you will search for answers to your questions. If this is a long-term plan, include a time line for each step.
1	
2	
3	
4	

CARRYING OUT THE PLAN

The Answers Summarize what you learned. Include the source of information and identify the question (by number) that it helps answer.		
Summary of Information	**Source**	**Question**

Classroom Tools

IDENTIFYING FURTHER LEARNING OPPORTUNITIES

Evaluating My Success
Identify how well you think you answered all of your questions by checking the statements that describe the results of your learning plan.

☐ All of my questions were answered completely.
☐ Most of my questions were answered.
☐ Only a few of my questions were answered.
☐ I asked the right questions.
☐ There are better questions that I could have asked to learn about the topic more thoroughly.
☐ My search for answers generated more questions about the topic.
☐ The sources of information I used were helpful.
☐ I had to find new sources to thoroughly answer my questions.

Questions for Further Study
What questions might be used in future investigations about this topic?

1	
2	
3	
4	
5	

Classroom Tools

Point, Counterpoint

Learning and Innovation Skills	Information, Media, and Technology Skills	Life and Career Skills (Check those to be addressed)
○ Creativity and Innovation ✓ Critical Thinking and Problem Solving ✓ Communication ✓ Collaboration	○ Information Literacy ○ Media Literacy ○ Information, Communications, and Technology Literacy	☐ Flexibility and Adaptability ☐ Initiative and Self-Direction ☐ Social and Cross-Cultural Skills ☐ Productivity and Accountability ☐ Leadership and Responsibility

In this tool, students practice looking at the different sides of a controversial issue.

HOW TO USE THIS TOOL

1. Present students with an issue related to the topic they have been studying, or have students select an issue of their own. The issue should allow for differing perspectives or be of a controversial nature.

2. Explain the need to look at both sides of the issue.

3. Students enter reasons that people might be in favor of the issue in the left-hand column of the graphic organizer and reasons that people might be opposed to the issue in the right-hand column.

4. Students can use the completed graphic organizer as the basis for class discussion, debates, or a persuasive presentation that presents the case for favoring or opposing the issue.

TIPS FOR USING THIS TOOL

• Model the thinking process with a topic that students have already studied.

• Conduct a class discussion on bias prior to conducting the activity. Help students understand how people might have different perspectives on an issue.

• Discuss the difficulties in seeing another side to an issue when you feel strongly one way or another about a topic. Stress the importance of trying to see an issue from multiple perspectives or viewpoints and how people's backgrounds and experiences might affect their views.

Classroom Tools

- Discuss ways that two people can disagree respectfully. Consider modeling or simulating a conversation in which two people are discussing an issue about which they have conflicting views.

USING TECHNOLOGY

- Set up a blog post where students can share their viewpoints on the issue. Students could be required to post comments that consider both perspectives of the issue. Evaluate students on the clarity of their comments as well as how respectfully they present them.
- Students can enter their reasons for either supporting or opposing the issue into an online collaboration tool.
- Create a wiki that encompasses both sides of the issue and into which students can compile resources for further investigation.
- Have students create a multimedia presentation that supports one side of an issue.
- Create an online survey that students can send to others to solicit reasons for favoring or opposing the issue. Students can use the results to help frame their arguments.

THINKING IT THROUGH

You can address these questions during class discussion, in small groups, in student journals, or in a variety of other ways.

- Why is it important for you to be able to think about both sides of an issue? How did your own biases affect your ability to see both sides?
- Explain the thinking process you used to try to process the issue from opposite viewpoints. What made it difficult to view the issue from a perspective that was different than your own?
- What criteria did you use to judge the quality of your reasons? Were your reasons logical and supportable with evidence?
- Think of examples or rules of how you could respectfully communicate with someone who has an opinion that is different than your own.

Classroom Tools

Point, Counterpoint

In the arrows on the left-hand side, list reasons someone might be in favor of the issue. In the arrows on the right-hand side, list an opposite perspective that would lead someone to be opposed to the issue.

Issue: _____

Reasons for Being in Favor of the Issue	Reasons for Opposing the Issue

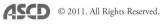

Classroom Tools

Preparing, Engaging, and Applying My Learning

Learning and Innovation Skills	Information, Media, and Technology Skills	Life and Career Skills (Check those to be addressed)
✓ Creativity and Innovation ✓ Critical Thinking and Problem Solving ○ Communication ○ Collaboration	○ Information Literacy ○ Media Literacy ○ Information, Communications, and Technology Literacy	☐ Flexibility and Adaptability ☐ Initiative and Self-Direction ☐ Social and Cross-Cultural Skills ☐ Productivity and Accountability ☐ Leadership and Responsibility

This tool walks students through the three stages of learning something new: preparing to learn, engaging your thinking as you learn, and applying what you have learned.

HOW TO USE THIS TOOL

1. Discuss the importance of continually processing and thinking about what you are learning.
2. Students complete the first two columns under "Preparing to Learn."
   - They brainstorm what they already know or think they know about the topic ("Getting Ready").
   - They create a list of what they need to know to understand the topic ("Thinking Ahead").
3. As students engage in the learning, they complete the two columns under "Engaging My Thinking" by listing their new learning about the topic and by developing questions that they still have about the topic.
4. After completing their study, students note in the "Applying What I Learned" column how their new learning applies to their own lives or to other studies.
5. Provide students with opportunities to share information from each column during a whole-class or small-group discussion.

TIPS FOR USING THIS TOOL

- Encourage students to list anything that they think they know or understand prior to the learning activity. Stress that they should include information even if they are not certain about it, because this will help them identify misconceptions as they continue the learning process.

Classroom Tools

- In the "New Learning" column, students should enter only new concepts and understandings. The information under that heading should reflect the added value of the learning and how the learning has increased their knowledge base.
- Questions students develop can be of two types:
  1. Questions that reflect what is not understood and needs to be clarified.
  2. Questions that indicate the need or desire for more information that was not included in the learning activity.
- After students individually complete each phase of the process, they can share their information in small groups.

USING TECHNOLOGY

- Create a table or spreadsheet that includes each of the five columns and post it on an online collaboration site. Have students work in small groups or individually to enter their information into each column, using a specific font color.
- Have students conduct an Internet search on the topic they will be studying. Have them review several promising websites, scanning through them by paying attention to titles, pictures, charts, graphs, captions, and subheadings (see "Picking the Right Site" on page 127) to provide an overview of the types of information that is available on the topic. The overview will help them recall what they already know, build some background knowledge, and develop a cognitive structure for organizing the information as they learn.
- Post questions that students generate on a blog or online collaboration tool and have classmates or students from other classes respond to their questions.
- Consider using a website such as Ask.com to search for answers to questions and review websites that might provide answers.

THINKING IT THROUGH

You can address these questions during class discussion, in small groups, in student journals, or in a variety of other ways.

- How does thinking about what you already know or think you know about a topic help prepare you to learn about it? Give an example.
- How did you develop the list of what you need to know? Describe how you chose the topics or questions that you included in the section "Thinking Ahead."
- How did you decide what constituted new learning? Why might it be important for you to separate new learning from what you already knew?

Classroom Tools

- Which column was the most difficult for you to complete? Why? Do you think that this will always be the case, or do you think it will vary based on the topic?
- How can you apply these phases of thinking to other learning situations?

Preparing, Engaging, and Applying My Learning

Learning about something new involves three stages: preparing to learn, engaging your thinking as you learn, and applying what you have learned.

1. Start your investigation by noting what you already know and what you think you will need to know to really understand the topic.
2. As you learn about the topic, make notes about new ideas you have learned and questions that are unanswered.
3. When you've finished with your investigation, note how you think you can apply what you have learned.

Preparing to Learn		Engaging My Thinking		Applying What I Learned
Getting Ready What do you already know or think you know about the topic?	**Thinking Ahead** What do you think you need to know to understand the topic?	**New Learning** What new understandings or ideas did you learn about the topic?	**Questions** What questions do you have still have about the topic?	**So What?** What have you learned that you can apply to your own life or future study?

Classroom Tools

Processing the Data

Learning and Innovation Skills	Information, Media, and Technology Skills	Life and Career Skills (Check those to be addressed)
✓ Creativity and Innovation ✓ Critical Thinking and Problem Solving ✓ Communication ○ Collaboration	✓ Information Literacy ○ Media Literacy ○ Information, Communications, and Technology Literacy	☐ Flexibility and Adaptability ☐ Initiative and Self-Direction ☐ Social and Cross-Cultural Skills ☐ Productivity and Accountability ☐ Leadership and Responsibility

In this tool, students practice making inferences based on a text and their own background knowledge.

HOW TO USE THIS TOOL

1. Explain to students what an inference is: a conclusion drawn by combining different pieces of information from the text with information from our own experiences; it is not stated directly by the author.

2. Help students understand how to make inferences or draw conclusions by modeling the process. Remind them that a good inference may not always correct, but it does have enough evidence to logically support it. For example, if a car has its right turn signal on, it is a good inference that the car will be turning right. But that doesn't always happen!

3. Determine if students should make inferences first and then support them with evidence or if they should gather data first from which they can make inferences.

4. Assign a reading to students, instructing them to focus on inferences and supporting evidence that emerges.

5. Students list
   - Inferences they made from the reading in the top box of the graphic organizer.
   - Evidence from the text in the left-hand box.
   - Evidence from their own experience or knowledge base in the right-hand box.

6. Ask students to share their inferences and supporting evidence.

TIPS FOR USING THIS TOOL

- Students should be prepared to support their inferences.
- Students could work in small groups to share their inferences and evidence and combine ideas into new or revised inferences.

• Encourage students to draw on previous instruction or units for support for their inferences.

USING TECHNOLOGY

• Students can locate information to support or build on their inferences from an Internet search. Remind students that they should check the credibility of their sources before using any information (see "Picking the Right Site" on page 127).

• Have students construct a PowerPoint slide or presentation to share their inferences and supporting evidence.

• Ask students to create a visual presentation on how to make a good inference.

THINKING IT THROUGH

You can address these questions during class discussion, in small groups, in student journals, or in a variety of other ways.

• Give several examples of how you make inferences in everyday life.

• How did you determine when you had enough evidence to support your inference? Do you think others would agree with you? Why or why not?

• What might be the drawbacks of jumping to conclusions or making inferences without enough information? Give an example of a time you or someone else did this and what the result was.

• Explain how being able to make good inferences can help you become a better learner.

Classroom Tools

 143

Processing the Data

By combining different pieces of information from the text with information from our own experiences, we can form conclusions or make inferences about what we have learned. These conclusions are supported by evidence from the text itself or our own prior knowledge, but they are not stated directly by the author.

As you read the selection, think about some reasonable conclusions you might reach about the subject. Select one such conclusion or inference and write it below. Then enter the text evidence and data from your own experience that support your inference.

Conclusion or Inference:	
Support from the Text	**Support from My Own Experience**

Putting It into Perspective

Learning and Innovation Skills	Information, Media, and Technology Skills	Life and Career Skills (Check those to be addressed)
○ Creativity and Innovation ✓ Critical Thinking and Problem Solving ✓ Communication ✓ Collaboration	○ Information Literacy ○ Media Literacy ○ Information, Communications, and Technology Literacy	☐ Flexibility and Adaptability ☐ Initiative and Self-Direction ☐ Social and Cross-Cultural Skills ☐ Productivity and Accountability ☐ Leadership and Responsibility

In this tool, students consider divergent opinions, predict the rationale for both sides, conduct interviews to verify their predictions, and reflect on how expectations can influence their communication with others.

HOW TO USE THIS TOOL

1. Identify a problem or issue that will be the focus of the activity. You can also have individual students or groups of students select their own problem or issue related to the topic of study.

2. Students note their personal opinions about the problem or issue.

3. Students predict what someone with the opposite viewpoint might say about the problem or issue.

4. Students reflect on what two opposing sides might agree on or have in common relating to the problem or issue.

5. Students reflect on potential differences among those who have the same viewpoint.

6. Students conduct two interviews:

   • One with a person who agrees with them.

   • One with someone who does not hold the same opinions about the issue or problem.

7. Students reflect on how their expectations matched the results of their interviews.

8. Conduct a class discussion about how expectations about differing viewpoints or perspectives affect communication.

Classroom Tools

 ☐ 145

TIPS FOR USING THIS TOOL

• Establish students' level of prior knowledge about the issue or problem. It may be necessary to provide some background knowledge about the issue or problem before using the tool. You can use the tool as a culminating activity for a unit of study.

• Before the activity, discuss the importance of looking at issues from many perspectives.

• Consider having students interview others outside of the classroom.

• Ask students to take notes during or after their interviews that summarize the discussion.

• Students might work in pairs to complete the activity and interviews.

• Working in pairs, each student could take different sides of the same issue, and students could interview each other.

USING TECHNOLOGY

• Use video conferencing, such as Skype, to have students interview others outside of the school setting. If the interviewee is someone who is an expert in the field, the interview could be broadcast to the class as a whole.

• Create a blog post about the issue and seek input from others who have different perspectives. The blog can help build background knowledge leading up to the activity.

• Create a video of the interviews students conduct. After sharing their videos, allow the creators to respond to questions from classmates. Videos can be uploaded to a secure site for future reference.

• Summarize the two interviews with a multimedia presentation that presents both sides of the issue or problem.

THINKING IT THROUGH

You can address these questions during class discussion, in small groups, in student journals, or in a variety of other ways.

• How did anticipating another person's arguments help you prepare for a conversation with him or her?

• How can you share your personal opinion while being respectful of a another's point of view?

• Give an example of how the opinion of someone who mostly agrees with you on an issue could still differ in some respects from your own opinion.

• Did you change your mind about any aspect of the issue or problem as a result of discussing it with others? Give an example.

Putting It into Perspective

To fully understand a problem or issue, it is important to examine it from as many viewpoints as possible—including our own! Think through each of the following questions and make notes of your answers in the right-hand column.

Issue or Problem: _____

_____

Question	My Answer
What is your personal opinion about the issue or problem? What are your ideas about how to solve the problem?	
What do you think someone opposed to your viewpoint would say about the issue or problem?	
What might both you and someone who disagreed with you have in common? What can you both agree about?	
In what areas might you differ with people who mostly agree with you?	

Interview at least one person who mostly agrees with you and one person who mostly disagrees with you about the issue. Compare their comments to your answers above.

Classroom Tools

 147

Questioning the Topic

Learning and Innovation Skills	Information, Media, and Technology Skills	Life and Career Skills (Check those to be addressed)
✓ Creativity and Innovation ✓ Critical Thinking and Problem Solving ○ Communication ○ Collaboration	✓ Information Literacy ○ Media Literacy ○ Information, Communications, and Technology Literacy	☐ Flexibility and Adaptability ☐ Initiative and Self-Direction ☐ Social and Cross-Cultural Skills ☐ Productivity and Accountability ☐ Leadership and Responsibility

This tool gives students practice in creating high-quality questions about a topic.

HOW TO USE THIS TOOL

1. Lead a class discussion about how to identify high-quality questions that are important to the topic being studied. High-quality questions are those that lead to a deep understanding of the topic and that cause the person answering them to use higher-order thinking skills.

2. Working individually, in pairs, or in small groups, students craft questions that they believe are important to understanding the topic.

3. Approve the questions that students have generated before giving them time to answer them.

4. Students answer the questions using either the resources you have provided or finding their own resources.

5. Use the students' questions as the foundation for class discussions.

TIPS FOR USING THIS TOOL

• Consider having students evaluate one another's questions and rate their quality. They should include suggestions for improvement.

• Individual students, pairs, or groups could exchange and answer one another's questions.

• If students answer their own questions, they should also be prepared to present their questions and answers with the rest of the class.

• You can record students' questions on note cards and have students draw to determine the question that they will use as the focus for their research or study.

USING TECHNOLOGY

• If students use the Internet to search for answers, they should cite the source of the information they find (such as the URL of the website).
• Have students brainstorm a list of key words or phrases they might use to find answers on the Internet.
• Post students' questions on a collaborative online writing tool and have students respond to one another's questions.
• If students use the Internet for research, have them contribute their sources to a social bookmarking site and include a brief annotation of the site.

THINKING IT THROUGH

You can address these questions during class discussion, in small groups, in student journals, or in a variety of other ways.

• How difficult was it to create high-quality questions? What criteria did you apply in judging the quality of your questions?
• How does the importance of the question affect the amount of detail or time that you should spend answering it?
• How does developing questions help direct your thinking or understanding of the topic?

Classroom Tools

Questioning the Topic

Brainstorm questions that might be asked about the topic you are studying. Identify three important questions that need to be answered before you begin your learning. Research the questions to identify answers.

Topic of inquiry: _____

Question 1	Question 2	Question 3
Answer	**Answer**	**Answer**

Classroom Tools

Questions in Search of Answers

Learning and Innovation Skills	Information, Media, and Technology Skills	Life and Career Skills (Check those to be addressed)
○ Creativity and Innovation ✓ Critical Thinking and Problem Solving ✓ Communication ✓ Collaboration	✓ Information Literacy ○ Media Literacy ○ Information, Communications, and Technology Literacy	☐ Flexibility and Adaptability ☐ Initiative and Self-Direction ☐ Social and Cross-Cultural Skills ☐ Productivity and Accountability ☐ Leadership and Responsibility

In this tool, students create four different types of questions and then research and share their answers.

HOW TO USE THIS TOOL

1. Explain the four types of questions in the activity:
   - **Point to It:** Questions that can be answered with facts.
   - **Put It Together:** Questions that require a generalization or comparison that puts together different pieces of information.
   - **Apply It:** Questions that require an answer that uses the knowledge or skill in a new situation or in a new way.
   - **Evaluate It:** Questions that require some kind of decision about the value or worth of the topic or concept.
2. As a class, develop at least one question for each category.
3. Students work in groups to develop more questions for each category. The questions can guide their search for information, or they can develop the questions from the information they find about the topic.
4. The questions can frame classroom or group discussions.

TIPS FOR USING THIS TOOL

- If you develop questions as a pre-instructional activity, students can select a question from each category to answer as they learn about the topic.
- You can divvy up the questions among group members so that each member of the group is responsible for researching and answering at least one question from each category. Students then share their findings with the rest of the group. Finally, the class as a whole can discuss any questions students are unsure about or want more information about.

- You can use questions for review or as summative test questions.
- Have students select one question that they will answer in the form of a presentation to the class. Encourage them to use visual images as well as text.
- Consider using the activity to connect ideas between topics that students have studied in separate units.
- If students are using information from the Internet to answer questions, remind them to check the validity and reliability of the sources they use (see "Picking the Right Site" on page 127).

USING TECHNOLOGY

- Post the questions that students generate on a blog post related to the topic. Students then add in the comments section the answers so that they can build on one another's work.
- Use a collaborative site, such as Google Docs or Stixy.com, to compile answers to each question.
- Each question can be used as the heading of a PowerPoint slide, and students can enter their answers onto the slides as they locate information.

THINKING IT THROUGH

You can address these questions during class discussion, in small groups, in student journals, or in a variety of other ways.

- Which types of questions were the hardest to create? Why?
- Do you think some of the types of questions lead to a greater understanding of the topic than others? Why?
- What clues from the text did you use to frame the questions? How can you use this same thinking process to locate answers to questions you have about other topics?

Questions in Search of Answers

Asking good questions, either before you learn about a topic or as you learn, helps build your understanding. Develop at least three questions for each of the four types described below.

Point to It Questions that can be answered with facts.	**Put It Together** Questions that require a generalization or comparison that puts together different pieces of information.
1. 2. 3.	1. 2. 3.
Apply It Questions that require an answer that uses the knowledge or skill in a new situation or in a new way.	**Evaluate It** Questions that require some kind of decision about the value or worth of the topic or concept.
1. 2. 3.	1. 2. 3.

Classroom Tools

Reflecting on My Learning

Learning and Innovation Skills	Information, Media, and Technology Skills	Life and Career Skills (Check those to be addressed)
○ Creativity and Innovation ✓ Critical Thinking and Problem Solving ○ Communication ○ Collaboration	✓ Information Literacy ○ Media Literacy ○ Information, Communications, and Technology Literacy	☐ Flexibility and Adaptability ☐ Initiative and Self-Direction ☐ Social and Cross-Cultural Skills ☐ Productivity and Accountability ☐ Leadership and Responsibility

This tool helps students reflect on their learning by summarizing, making connections with prior knowledge, and asking questions.

HOW TO USE THIS TOOL

1. Either provide students with a variety of sources of information or have them locate at least four sources of information they can use to learn about a topic.
2. Discuss each category on the form with students so that they have a clear understanding of what each means.
    - **Main points** are the important understandings or conclusions that they draw from the information and that are supported with evidence.
    - **Connections** include how they have applied the information or how they connect the information with something they already knew or from another source.
    - **Questions** can be those that require clarification for understanding or that request information that is not included in the source.
3. Students write the name or location of each source of information in the top of each section of the graphic organizer.
4. Students review the sources of information and reflect on what they have learned by completing the three categories for each source.
5. Ask students to share what they learned in small groups or in a class discussion.

TIPS FOR USING THIS TOOL

- You could have students present a summary that incorporates information from each of the sources.
- Students can work in groups of four, with each student processing one of the sources. Then the group members share their main points, connections, and questions with the

Classroom Tools

group. After each student has shared, the group can discern major points or ideas that have emerged from across all of the sources.

• Students can share their work on chart paper that is posted on the walls of the classroom. Traveling in small groups, students do a gallery walk, during which they review one another's information and look for common ideas and themes.

USING TECHNOLOGY

• Post the form on an online collaboration site and allow all students who are using the same source of information to contribute ideas to the form. Students can use unique font colors to identify their individual contributions.

• Students can use an online annotation tool, such as Diigo, to highlight and save important passages from online text and share them with other students.

• Create a table or spreadsheet that incorporates columns for the sources of information, the main points, connections, and questions. Have students enter their finished work into the table or spreadsheet, and then post it to a common online site for students' reflection and review.

THINKING IT THROUGH

You can address these questions during class discussion, in small groups, in student journals, or in a variety of other ways.

• How did you determine the main points from each source of information? Explain the criteria you used to determine what made it important.

• Why is making connections between what you already know and the new information important for understanding an idea or concept?

• How can developing questions about what you are studying help you learn?

• Which of the three categories of information (main points, connections, and questions) was most difficult for you to complete? Why?

Reflecting on My Learning

After reviewing each source of information, reflect on what you have learned. Make notes in each section below about the main points you have learned, connections you have made to what you already knew, and questions you still have about the information.

Source 1:	Source 2:
Main Points: Connections: Questions:	Main Points: Connections: Questions:
Source 3:	**Source 4:**
Main Points: Connections: Questions:	Main Points: Connections: Questions:

Classroom Tools

Remote Control Thinking

Learning and Innovation Skills	Information, Media, and Technology Skills	Life and Career Skills (Check those to be addressed)
✓ Creativity and Innovation ○ Critical Thinking and Problem Solving ✓ Communication ○ Collaboration	✓ Information Literacy ○ Media Literacy ○ Information, Communications, and Technology Literacy	☐ Flexibility and Adaptability ☐ Initiative and Self-Direction ☐ Social and Cross-Cultural Skills ☐ Productivity and Accountability ☐ Leadership and Responsibility

In this tool, students think through a topic they are going to present to the class using the analogy of the buttons on a remote control to narrow down their main focus.

HOW TO USE THIS TOOL

1. Give students 1–3 minutes to list as many words or phrases they can think of that are related to the topic. They should record their list in the "Play" area.

2. Students review their lists and select three words that are of greatest interest to them or that they have the most questions about.

3. For each of the words they choose, students generate additional words or phrases related to the topic. They should record this list in the "Pause" area. Provide students approximately three minutes for this portion of the activity.

4. Students select one more word from their "Play" list and generate additional words and phrases connected to their choice. They should record this list in the "Rewind" area.

5. Students review all of their work to this point and look for repeated words or similar words or ideas. From this review, they pick two ideas that appear most often and write them in the "Fast Forward" section.

6. Students select one of their main ideas and continue to list new words and phrases associated with it that they could use when talking or writing about the idea. They should record this list in the "Change Channels" area.

7. Students compare the list of words across the "Change Channels," "Play," and "Pause" areas and record repeated words, phrases, or ideas in the "Volume" section.

8. Students develop a presentation based on the main idea or focus derived from their list in the "Volume" section. Students can use words and phrases from across all of the categories to create their presentation.

Classroom Tools

9. In the "Record" area, students write the opening sentence for their presentations.

TIPS FOR USING THIS TOOL

• Discuss the concept of a main idea and how it is different than details. Provide students with examples from a previous unit of study or a topic relevant to their daily lives.

• Discuss the concept of writer's block and help students understand that it is not unusual for even professional writers to have trouble thinking about what to write or include in their message.

• Provide time limits for each section of the organizer, allowing students enough time to get ideas flowing but forcing them to think deeply and quickly.

• Students could work in pairs or small groups on the activity to generate more ideas. They can then either work on their presentation alone or continue to work in pairs or small groups.

• Encourage students to write down everything that comes to mind when they are working in the "Play," "Pause," and "Rewind" sections. The purpose of these steps is to get as many ideas as possible.

• If students are all presenting on the same topic, have them keep a running record of common words and phrases that they hear repeated across presentations.

USING TECHNOLOGY

• Have students work in small groups and use an online document sharing program, such as Google Docs, to add words and phrases to each area of the graphic organizer. Students can then compare each group's results and process similarities and differences.

• Ask students to reflect on how they could use additional buttons of the remote control analogy to generate ideas.

• Allow students to use a wide variety of technologies in preparing their presentations. Ask them to include a list of the keywords or phrases generated from the activity that they used in the presentation.

THINKING IT THROUGH

You can address these questions during class discussion, in small groups, in student journals, or in a variety of other ways.

• Did thinking of words and phrases help you clarify the most important ideas or concepts about the topic? Why or why not?

- How could you use an activity similar to this one when you are preparing a presentation or writing about a topic? Give at least one example.
- Why do you think it was important to keep reviewing your previous thoughts as you moved forward?
- What are some other ways to unblock your thinking when you are writing or creating a presentation?

Remote Control Thinking

To develop a clear focus for your presentation or to avoid getting stuck when you are working on a presentation, consider periodically shifting your thinking, similar to how you would use a remote control for a television. Follow each function of the remote below as you prepare your presentation.

Topic: _____

REMOTE CONTROL FUNCTIONS

Play
Using a free flow of thoughts, list as many words and phrases as you can that relate to the topic.

Pause
Stop and review the list you created under "Play." Select three of the key words and use them as a springboard to think of even more words or phrases related to the topic.

Keyword 1:	Keyword 2:	Keyword 3:

Rewind
Review your original list of key words and phrases that you generated in the "Play" function. Choose one more word or phrase and do some more brainstorming of related words and ideas.

Classroom Tools

Fast Forward

Review the key words and phrases from all three previous functions, looking for repeated or similar words. Pick at least two main ideas that appear most often.

1.

2.

Change Channels

Pick one of the main ideas from your fast-forward review and create a new list of words and phrases you might use in your presentation.

Volume

Look at your new list of words and phrases in "Change Channels" and see if they match any that you included in your "Play" and "Pause" functions. List below any that match. These are probably key to understanding the topic.

Record

Prepare your presentation on the topic, using the main idea you identified in "Volume" as the focus and including as many of the key words and phrases as you can. Write your opening sentence or describe your opening scene in the space below and complete your presentation from there.

Respecting Different Perspectives

Learning and Innovation Skills	Information, Media, and Technology Skills	Life and Career Skills (Check those to be addressed)
○ Creativity and Innovation ✓ Critical Thinking and Problem Solving ✓ Communication ✓ Collaboration	○ Information Literacy ○ Media Literacy ○ Information, Communications, and Technology Literacy	☐ Flexibility and Adaptability ☐ Initiative and Self-Direction ☐ Social and Cross-Cultural Skills ☐ Productivity and Accountability ☐ Leadership and Responsibility

This tool can help students prepare for a conversation or interview with someone who has a different opinion about a controversial issue.

HOW TO USE THIS TOOL

1. Present students with an issue or problem related to the topic they have been studying.
2. Determine the person or group with whom the conversation about the topic would be conducted. This could be someone with a strong opinion or someone with substantial knowledge about the topic.
3. Discuss as a class each of the four questions and model the activity with a topic that students know well.
4. Students respond to each of the four questions in the graphic organizer to prepare for a real or simulated conversation with the identified person or group.
5. Students conduct a real or simulated interview with the person or group selected in step 2.
6. Ask students to reflect on how their preparation resulted in a better conversation with the other person or group.

TIPS FOR USING THIS TOOL

• Consider allowing individuals or groups of students to select the topic or problem for this activity.
• Students could use this tool to prepare for an interview with someone outside of the classroom or with a peer. Have students summarize the results of the interview or conversation.
• Have students exchange their work with a peer for review and for further suggestions.
• Students can work in small groups to conduct the activity.

Classroom Tools

• You can eliminate steps 5 and 6 if the purpose of the activity is to help students learn how to think about different perspectives on a topic.

USING TECHNOLOGY

• Create a video of the students interviewing another person about this topic. Students can use the video for self-assessment and reflection.

• As a class, watch professional television interviews and have students identify how the interviewers show respect for the person they are interviewing in their body language as well as comments. Point out how the interviewer respectfully poses questions.

• Have students interview an expert in the field via the Internet, either through a blog or e-mail exchange. If available, consider using Skye or some other visual conferencing tool for the interview.

THINKING IT THROUGH

You can address these questions during class discussion, in small groups, in student journals, or in a variety of other ways.

• Which of the questions was most difficult for you to complete? Why?

• Why is it important to respect others' ideas and opinions? How does showing respect improve communication?

• How do you feel when your ideas or opinions are not acknowledged? Give an example of when this happened to you.

• What actions show the most respect for another person's ideas or opinions?

• How could you have better demonstrated respect for others? What specific actions could you use to show respect for others?

Classroom Tools

Respecting Different Perspectives

Communicating with people who have different perspectives about an issue or problem can be difficult. Prepare for your conversation by answering the following questions.

Topic: _____

Person or Group: _____

1. How do you think this person feels about the topic?

2. What experiences or factors do you think might have shaped this person's perspective?

3. What questions do you want to ask?

4. What actions on your part will show that you acknowledge and respect the other person's ideas or opinions?

Round-Robin Ideas

Learning and Innovation Skills	Information, Media, and Technology Skills	Life and Career Skills (Check those to be addressed)
✓ Creativity and Innovation ✓ Critical Thinking and Problem Solving ✓ Communication ✓ Collaboration	○ Information Literacy ○ Media Literacy ○ Information, Communications, and Technology Literacy	☐ Flexibility and Adaptability ☐ Initiative and Self-Direction ☐ Social and Cross-Cultural Skills ☐ Productivity and Accountability ☐ Leadership and Responsibility

Students can use this tool to help brainstorm possible solutions to a problem and, after weighing many possible options, choose the one that would best solve the problem.

HOW TO USE THIS TOOL

1. Identify a problem to be solved or allow students to determine a problem associated with the topic being studied.
2. Establish an order for students to take turns providing possible solutions to the problem.
3. Explain that no idea is good or bad at this point, and encourage students to be creative in their thinking.
4. Each student, in order, suggests an idea or possible solution. Record their ideas on chart paper or in a document that is projected where all can see it.
    - Students are not allowed to comment, either positively or negatively, about the ideas.
    - Student can pass if they have nothing to contribute, but they have the chance to add new ideas each round as their turn comes up.
    - Continue to ask for ideas until every person has passed.
5. Students break into groups of 3–4 to review the ideas and select what they believe are the three best ideas.
6. Each group shares their best three ideas. Tally their responses on the chart paper or projected document.
7. Circle or highlight the five most popular ideas from the groups' collective responses.
8. Students work in their small groups to identify the merits of each of the top five ideas, discussing the pros and cons of each.

9. As a class use another round-robin session to share the pros and cons of each idea. Record these on the graphic organizer either on chart paper or a projected chart.

10. Use a consensus-building process (see "Developing Consensus" on page 87) to identify the top two ideas or solutions.

11. Small groups discuss the possible implementation of each idea.

12. Each small group shares its implementation ideas. Each group can then select one of the ideas to further develop and carry out.

TIPS FOR USING THIS TOOL

• You may need to give students guidelines or parameters for evaluating the ideas. However, be careful that these do not limit their thinking. They should give students ways of expanding their thinking about the pros and cons of each idea.

• Enforce the rule that students are not allowed to voice opinions, positive or negative, about the ideas as they are presented. The goal is to be neutral about ideas until they are all shared.

• Share the concept of an idea offered by one student sparking an idea for another student. You should encourage this kind of idea progression and, when it happens, point it out as a benefit of collaboration.

• Push students to think deeply, exploring all aspects of the problem or issue and its potential solutions or ideas. Sometimes the best ideas are those that emerge after a great deal of consideration and thought.

• Encourage students to take a seemingly silly idea and rework it into something that has potential. This reworking can be part of the small-group discussions in selecting top ideas or can be a whole-group discussion before students break into their small group.

USING TECHNOLOGY

• Small groups can brainstorm solutions using an online collaboration tool, such as Google Docs. As they enter ideas, all groups can see them, which encourages students to build on one another's ideas and increases participation.

• Project a word processing document throughout the activity that includes all the ideas that students offer so that they can review them.

• During their group work, ask students to enter their ideas into an electronic table, which they can e-mail to another group for reflection and to spur new ideas.

• Students can use a blog to enter ideas about pros and cons. Every student should be responsible for contributing at least one pro and one con for each idea.

THINKING IT THROUGH

You can address these questions during class discussion, in small groups, in student journals, or in a variety of other ways.

• Why is it important to withhold judgment about an idea until all of the possibilities have been suggested?

• How might you use this process in other areas of your life? Give at least one example.

• How did the group come to a consensus about the final two ideas or solutions? What did the group do to ensure that everyone supported the selections?

• Why is it important to examine both the positives and negatives of an idea? What further insights came to light from doing so? In what kinds of situations might looking at both the pros and cons of an issue be important?

• Why is it important to take turns in generating ideas? What was helpful about doing it this way? What was not?

Classroom Tools

Round-Robin Ideas

1. BRAINSTORMING

In the left-hand column, list in any order the five most promising ideas that the group has agreed on. Then consider the pros and cons of each idea.

Our Group's Top Five Ideas	Pros	Cons

2. ACTING ON IDEAS

For the top two ideas that you agreed on as a class, discuss how you could go about implementing them.

Top Two Ideas	Potential for Implementation

Support It and Share It

Learning and Innovation Skills	Information, Media, and Technology Skills	Life and Career Skills (Check those to be addressed)
○ Creativity and Innovation ✓ Critical Thinking and Problem Solving ✓ Communication ✓ Collaboration	✓ Information Literacy ✓ Media Literacy ○ Information, Communications, and Technology Literacy	☐ Flexibility and Adaptability ☐ Initiative and Self-Direction ☐ Social and Cross-Cultural Skills ☐ Productivity and Accountability ☐ Leadership and Responsibility

In this tool, students practice gathering evidence to support a generalization, principle, or opinion and then share their work with the class.

HOW TO USE THIS TOOL

1. Identify a generalization, principle, or opinion about the topic being studied. Students might also generate this after studying a topic for a period of time.

2. Students use information they have learned to identify evidence or examples that support the generalization, principle, or opinion. If students feel that they do not have enough or significant evidence, they can locate additional information and examples until they feel they have enough to strongly support it.

3. Students should cite the source of the evidence or examples, even if they are from their own experience.

4. Students prepare a presentation of their evidence to share with the rest of the class or with a small group.

TIPS FOR USING THIS TOOL

• Model the activity with a generalization or principle with which students are already familiar. This could be a previous topic of study or something from their everyday lives. Stress the need to adequately support the generalization or principle to make a strong case for it.

• Students can work individually, in small groups, or as a whole class on the activity.

• Students can generate generalizations or opinions from studying a variety of sources of information. Students can generate these as a whole class using a brainstorming process.

• If the generalization is appropriate across several units of study, consider posting a collection of evidence on an ongoing basis.

Classroom Tools

• Students can work backwards through the organizer, collecting examples and evidence first and then creating a generalization or opinion based on this information.

• Allow students to use a variety of presentation modes to share their information.

USING TECHNOLOGY

• If students use online sources of information, make sure that they assess the credibility of the sources (see "Picking the Right Site" on page 127).

• Students can collaboratively build their evidence and examples with an electronic tool, such as Google Docs.

• Allow students to use a wide variety of electronic tools to create their presentations.

THINKING IT THROUGH

You can address these questions during class discussion, in small groups, in student journals, or in a variety of other ways.

• How did you determine whether information supported the generalization or opinion? What criteria did you use?

• Describe the process you used to select the examples and evidence. How did you determine what to include?

• Do you think your examples and evidence strongly support the generalization or opinion? Why or why not?

Support It and Share It

List the facts, information, and examples that support the statement below. Cite the source for each. Make sure that you have enough evidence to form a strong basis of support. Then create a way to share your information with others or the class. Make it interesting as well as informative.

Generalization, Principle, or Opinion: _____

_____

Evidence	Source

Supporting Evidence

Learning and Innovation Skills	Information, Media, and Technology Skills	Life and Career Skills (Check those to be addressed)
○ Creativity and Innovation ✓ Critical Thinking and Problem Solving ✓ Communication ✓ Collaboration	✓ Information Literacy ○ Media Literacy ✓ Information, Communications, and Technology Literacy	☐ Flexibility and Adaptability ☐ Initiative and Self-Direction ☐ Social and Cross-Cultural Skills ☐ Productivity and Accountability ☐ Leadership and Responsibility

In this tool, students gather supporting evidence for a generalization or opinion and then assess the validity of the statement.

HOW TO USE THIS TOOL

1. Students work in small groups to make several generalizations or form some opinion statements about the topic they are studying.
2. As each group reports on their generalizations or opinions, record them in a common document. Students should not discuss any of the suggestions at this time.
3. Each small group selects one of the generalizations or opinions as the topic for their research.
4. Using at least two sources of information, students identify examples or evidence that support the generalization or opinion they have chosen.
5. Based on their research, the group determines how valid the generalization or opinion is on a scale from 1–5:

   - 1 = Almost no support for it.
   - 5 = High support.

   The greater the question about the validity of the statement, the lower the score.
6. Each group presents their findings to the rest of the class.

TIPS FOR USING THIS TOOL

- Before this activity, conduct a class discussion about the need to support opinions and generalizations with facts. Consider using an example from a previous unit as a model.
- Have each group use a tool such as Google Docs to record their ideas. Such collaborative tools allow groups to see one another's work as they create it and may lead to ideas that build on one another. It will also eliminate the time needed to record students' ideas collectively.

• Small groups can record their ideas on chart paper as a method of reporting. The class can then use each group's work to create a master list of ideas for generalizations and opinions.

• If the generalization or opinion is broad, students can continue to add more examples or evidence across several units of study.

• Consider using the process in reverse, by having students first locate evidence on a topic and then develop the generalization or opinion from the evidence.

USING TECHNOLOGY

• If students are using the Internet as a source of information, remind them to assess the credibility of the sources they choose by examining the author's purpose or bias (see "Picking the Right Site" on page 127).

• Use online tools to enter research notes collaboratively.

• Ask students to present their findings visually, using appropriate media and technology tools.

THINKING IT THROUGH

You can address these questions during class discussion, in small groups, in student journals, or in a variety of other ways.

• Describe your process for selecting the sources of information you used to support the generalization or opinion.

• How did you handle conflicting information? Describe the criteria you used to determine whether or not you would include information in your final report.

• Did your group always agree about the validity of the information? Why might different people have different opinions? How did your group come to a consensus about the validity of ideas?

• Do you think your findings were convincing or complete? Why or why not? What could you have included that would have created stronger support for the generalization or opinion you were researching?

Classroom Tools

ASCD   173

Supporting Evidence

1. BRAINSTORM

Brainstorm several generalizations or opinions about the topic being studied. List them below and then put a checkmark by the one that you will support with research.

Generalizations or Opinions

2. RESEARCH

Find at least two sources of information where you will search for evidence or examples to support your generalization or opinion. List each source below and keep track of your evidence in the appropriate column. Then rate each piece of evidence on a scale of 1–5:

    1 = No support.

    5 = High support.

Source 1:	How Valid? (1–5)	Source 2:	How Valid? (1–5)

3. SUMMARIZE

Explain whether you feel your evidence or examples adequately support your generalization or opinion. Prepare a presentation to share with the class.

The Pros and Cons

Learning and Innovation Skills	Information, Media, and Technology Skills	Life and Career Skills (Check those to be addressed)
○ Creativity and Innovation ✓ Critical Thinking and Problem Solving ✓ Communication ✓ Collaboration	✓ Information Literacy ○ Media Literacy ○ Information, Communications, and Technology Literacy	☐ Flexibility and Adaptability ☐ Initiative and Self-Direction ☐ Social and Cross-Cultural Skills ☐ Productivity and Accountability ☐ Leadership and Responsibility

In this tool, students research the pros and cons of an issue and, based on their evidence, decide whether it's overall more positive or negative.

HOW TO USE THIS TOOL

1. Select an idea or issue related to the topic that has both positives and negatives. If possible, include students in the selection process. Enter a summary of the idea or issue in the first part of the organizer.

2. Working in small groups, students develop a set of subtopics or various aspects of the idea and list them in the center column of the chart.

3. Students research the topic and find evidence about each aspect and record it as either a positive or negative. If evidence can be perceived as both positive and negative, they should include it in both columns.

4. After examining the pros and cons, each group should develop a position statement that clearly explains whether they think the idea is more positive or negative and why.

TIPS FOR USING THIS TOOL

• Whether something is positive or negative is often in the eye of the beholder, and views are often rooted in background knowledge or individual values and beliefs. Help students understand how to agree to disagree and value the insights and opinions of all group members (see "Respecting Different Perspectives" on page 162).

• Model the process with a familiar topic or situation before students start to work.

• You can compile the list of positives and negatives from across groups as a foundation for a whole-class discussion.

• The ideas students generate can form the foundation of a persuasive essay, a debate, or some other form of summary presentation.

Classroom Tools

• Students can work collaboratively in pairs or teams to identify both the pros and cons, or pairs or groups can focus on only one aspect and then pool their ideas with others.

• Remind students to assess the reliability of the information they find on the topic and to think through the biases of the author or source of the information.

USING TECHNOLOGY

• Ask students to create a list of key words or phrases that they could use in an Internet search.

• Have students locate websites that they think might be most useful in this activity by conducting a brief scan of the results of their search. Ask them to reflect on why they think those websites would yield good information (see "Picking the Right Site" on page 127).

THINKING IT THROUGH

You can address these questions during class discussion, in small groups, in student journals, or in a variety of other ways.

• Explain how two people can see the same information as being either positive or negative.

• Identify examples of how using a chart like this could help you make personal decisions.

• Why is it important to consider both the positives and negatives of an issue?

• Which was easier for you: thinking positively or thinking negatively?

The Pros and Cons

Evaluating both sides of an issue or decision is important in making good choices.

1. Begin by thinking about the various aspects of the issue and entering them into the middle column.
2. As you search for information on the issue, record both the positives and negatives about the various aspects in the appropriate columns.
3. After you have finished your research, summarize your findings.

Idea or Issue:		
Positives	**Aspects**	**Negatives**
Summary or Conclusion		

The Viewpoint

Learning and Innovation Skills	Information, Media, and Technology Skills	Life and Career Skills (Check those to be addressed)
○ Creativity and Innovation ✓ Critical Thinking and Problem Solving ✓ Communication ✓ Collaboration	✓ Information Literacy ○ Media Literacy ○ Information, Communications, and Technology Literacy	☐ Flexibility and Adaptability ☐ Initiative and Self-Direction ☐ Social and Cross-Cultural Skills ☐ Productivity and Accountability ☐ Leadership and Responsibility

In this tool, students put themselves into the mind-set of an assigned role and research the potential perspectives of that role.

HOW TO USE THIS TOOL

1. Define the concept students will investigate. Share it with students, providing enough background knowledge to help them develop a clear understanding of what it is.
2. Develop three or more roles—for an individual or a group—from which students can examine the concept. Students will be evaluating perspectives on the concept from the mind-set of the role they are assigned. You could allow students to select the role they will assume.
3. As students study the concept or topic, they take notes on what the person or group they represent would find interesting or important and what points this person would support or oppose.
4. After students have completed the study, break them into groups that include a student representing each role. Each student shares the perspectives they believe the person or group they represent would have about the topic or concept.
5. Conduct a class discussion about how an individual's perspectives could alter their understanding of information, using examples from students' work.

TIPS FOR USING THIS TOOL

• Ensure that students understand the concept of perspective and how it influences an individual's understanding of a topic or concept. Provide examples from the students' own lives and ask students to share some of their own examples.

• Ask students to look for similarities and differences in perspectives across the roles they have been assigned. This might be a starting point for a class discussion of the activity.

• Before students meet in their heterogeneous groups, have all students who have been assigned the same role meet to share their ideas.

• As a follow-up activity, students could write a position paper or presentation based on the perspective of the person or group they have been assigned.

USING TECHNOLOGY

• Create a blog post on the topic or concept and post a significant question. Students would develop names that reflect the groups they represent and respond to the question in their roles.

• Create a Google Doc, or some other online sharing tool, of the activity for each of the roles and have students enter their notes directly into it. Be sure to have each student identified as the contributor to ensure that all are participating.

THINKING IT THROUGH

You can address these questions during class discussion, in small groups, in student journals, or in a variety of other ways.

• How is assuming another's role or viewpoint difficult? What did you like about it? What did you not like about it?

• What was most difficult for you in responding to the questions from the viewpoint of your assumed role?

• Did this activity increase your awareness of how others think? Give examples.

• Give examples of when it might be important to see an issue from another person's perspective.

• What type of social skills does it take to be able to communicate with others who have different perspectives on issues? What skills do you do well? In what areas can you improve?

Classroom Tools

 179

The Viewpoint

You will be assigned a role or will select a person or group from whose perspective you will study the topic. As you learn more about the topic, concept, or issue, answer the following questions from that person's or group's perspective.

Topic: _____

Role (from the perspective of): _____

1. What does this person or group find interesting?

2. What does this person or group find important?

3. What does this person or group support?

4. What does this person or group oppose?

Classroom Tools

Think Before You Judge

Learning and Innovation Skills	Information, Media, and Technology Skills	Life and Career Skills (Check those to be addressed)
✓ Creativity and Innovation ✓ Critical Thinking and Problem Solving ✓ Communication ✓ Collaboration	✓ Information Literacy ○ Media Literacy ○ Information, Communications, and Technology Literacy	☐ Flexibility and Adaptability ☐ Initiative and Self-Direction ☐ Social and Cross-Cultural Skills ☐ Productivity and Accountability ☐ Leadership and Responsibility

In this tool, students practice considering multiple ideas or opinions before coming to a conclusion or judgment.

HOW TO USE THIS TOOL

1. In small groups or as a whole class, students brainstorm ideas related to the concept being studied that are controversial or for which there might be multiple perspectives. Students enter these ideas in the left column.

2. Encourage students to remain open-minded about the ideas or opinions as they are presented.

3. Students note their reactions to each of the ideas or opinions in the "My Reaction" column.

4. Students circle the idea or opinion that they believe represents the best idea, solution, or opinion.

5. Students generate one to three statements in their own words that reflect their overall thinking about the topic.

6. Working in pairs or small groups, students share their reactions and summaries with each other. Ask them to find points of agreement and disagreement and record these on their graphic organizers.

TIPS FOR USING THIS TOOL

• Consider giving students a pre-assigned perspective from which to complete the task. As they work through the activity, they would look for ideas and opinions that support the perspective they have been assigned, seeing it through the eyes of others (see "The Viewpoint" on page 178).

Classroom Tools

- Stress the importance of having a balanced perspective on important issues. Ask students to review the ideas and opinions they have brainstormed to determine if they believe they have examined all sides of the issue.

- As an added review, students can provide or find evidence that supports their chosen idea or opinion. If necessary, they can conduct a brief search for information within a specific amount of time.

- Use the information from the activity to launch a more structured, formal debate on the issue.

- Students can write a persuasive essay or editorial to support their ideas or positions.

- Ensure that all students in small groups or pairs have an equal opportunity to share their ideas.

- Consider having students reflect on their team and interpersonal skills in working with the small group (see the Working Together Rubric on page 197).

USING TECHNOLOGY

- Students can enter all brainstormed ideas directly into a spreadsheet or table and then give electronic copies to classmates to complete with their own reactions and summaries.

THINKING IT THROUGH

You can address these questions during class discussion, in small groups, in student journals, or in a variety of other ways.

- Give examples of when it might be helpful for you to refrain from reacting to or judging an idea too quickly.

- What were the benefits of waiting to express your reactions to ideas until after completing the brainstorming?

- Describe your interactions with small groups. What do you do well? What could you improve?

- What does *bias* mean? Why is it important to keep it in mind as you read about and learn from others?

Think Before You Judge

1. List all of the ideas or opinions of the group in the first column.
2. Think about each idea or opinion and write your reaction to it.
3. Share your reactions and summaries with the rest of the group. List the ideas or opinions the group agrees with and those the group disagrees with.

Topic: _____

Ideas or Opinions of the Group	My Reaction

Summary of My Thinking

 © 2011. All Rights Reserved.

Classroom Tools

SUMMARY OF GROUP DISCUSSION

We are in agreement about...	We disagree about...

Classroom Tools

Three-by-Three Research

Learning and Innovation Skills	Information, Media, and Technology Skills	Life and Career Skills (Check those to be addressed)
○ Creativity and Innovation ✓ Critical Thinking and Problem Solving ✓ Communication ○ Collaboration	✓ Information Literacy ○ Media Literacy ✓ Information, Communications, and Technology Literacy	☐ Flexibility and Adaptability ☐ Initiative and Self-Direction ☐ Social and Cross-Cultural Skills ☐ Productivity and Accountability ☐ Leadership and Responsibility

In this tool, students research answers to questions about a topic of study and synthesize information from multiple sources.

HOW TO USE THIS TOOL

1. Identify three key questions about the topic or have students develop them through a class discussion. The questions should lead students to answers that encompass the most important learning about the topic.
2. Ask students to individually identify what they already know or think they know about the answers to each question.
3. Assign students three sources of information, or let students locate them on their own, to use in finding answers to the questions. Students note potential answers from each of the sources in the appropriate spaces on the organizer.
4. After finishing their research and notes, students summarize the answer, using the information they have gleaned from all three sources.

TIPS FOR USING THIS TOOL

• You can break students into groups of three to complete the activity. Assign each student a different question to research and share or have each student use a different source to answer all three questions. The group members then compile their answers and complete the summary statement together.

• If students are selecting their own sources, discuss the need to check the credibility of the source before using the information.

• You could select one question for the activity, the class could determine a second question, and individual students could select a third question.

• The questions could become part of a summative evaluation at the end of the unit.

USING TECHNOLOGY

- Have all students enter their answers to the key questions in an online document, identifying themselves as the author. As students scan across all information about a question, ask them to identify repeated or common ideas.
- Ask students to create a PowerPoint presentation to address the answers to all three questions. Advise them to stress the biggest ideas in their presentation.

THINKING IT THROUGH

You can address these questions during class discussion, in small groups, in student journals, or in a variety of other ways.

- How did understanding or forming the questions help direct your search for answers? How can you apply this thinking to other topics you are studying?
- Describe the thought process you used to develop the questions. What was easiest about developing key questions? What was the most difficult?
- What are the qualities of a "good" question?
- Describe the thinking you used to select information from the sources that answered the questions.

Three-by-Three Research

1. Note what you already know or think you know about the answers to the three key questions.
2. Review three sources of information to find additional information that answers the questions.
3. Using information from the all of the sources, summarize the answer.

Topic:	Question 1:	Question 2:	Question 3:
What I already know or think I know			
Source 1:			
Source 2:			
Source 3:			

Summary of the Answer:

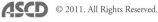

Using Primary Sources

Learning and Innovation Skills	Information, Media, and Technology Skills	Life and Career Skills: (Check those to be addressed)
○ Creativity and Innovation ✓ Critical Thinking and Problem Solving ✓ Communication ○ Collaboration	○ Information Literacy ✓ Media Literacy ○ Information, Communications, and Technology Literacy	☐ Flexibility and Adaptability ☐ Initiative and Self-Direction ☐ Social and Cross-Cultural Skills ☐ Productivity and Accountability ☐ Leadership and Responsibility

This tool helps students understand how to use and practice using primary resources to gather information.

HOW TO USE THIS TOOL

1. Explain the difference between primary and secondary sources of information.
    - **Primary sources** are created during the time period that students are studying. To understand a primary source, you must also understand the situation, event, or time period during which it was created.
    - **Secondary sources** are interpretations or reviews of the situation or events created by someone who did not have firsthand experience.
2. Choose a primary source that reflects directly on the learning objectives of the lesson.
3. Before giving students the primary source, ask them to reflect on what they already know about the topic, the creator, or the time period.
4. Provide background information about the primary source to fill in any gaps in students' prior knowledge. Give students enough information to help them understand the primary source. Students should complete the background section of the graphic organizer.
5. Students study the primary source and answer the questions in the inquiry section.
6. Students summarize what they have learned in the third section.

TIPS FOR USING THIS TOOL

- Primary sources could be documents, drawings, or speeches. Presented with the text of a speech as well as audio of it, students can reflect on how the spoken word influences the message. If a video of the primary source is as available, students can also reflect on how the added visuals affect their understanding and interpretation of the message.

• Consider providing students with a choice in the primary source they will be examining. You can give them two or three choices, or they can locate one of their own.

• If you provide multiple sources, the sources could reflect a diversity of opinions or insights. Students could compare the variety of perspectives and the reasons and biases of each.

• You can divide the class into groups, with each group analyzing a different primary source.

• Ask students to create their own secondary sources on the topic by writing an analysis of the primary source, presenting a speech, or developing a visual that summarizes its content.

• After students have completed their review of the primary source, have them review a secondary source that analyzes the primary source. Ask them to compare their own impressions with those expressed in the secondary source.

USING TECHNOLOGY

• Multiple websites are available that will provide text, audio, or visual primary sources. Consider searching major historical organizations, such as the Smithsonian and the Library of Congress. An Internet search of the topic will also yield primary sources.

• Create a wiki or other collaborative site to share information about the primary source.

• Have students use a collaborative writing tool to share their ideas and thoughts in a single document.

THINKING IT THROUGH

You can address these questions during class discussion, in small groups, in student journals, or in a variety of other ways.

• Why is it important to understand the author's viewpoint when using a primary source?

• Did examining the primary source change your opinion or understanding of the topic? In what ways?

• Think of an example in your own life of a time when getting firsthand information about something might be important.

• Can you support your analysis of the primary source with adequate reasoning and details? How effective do you think you were in your analysis?

Classroom Tools

Using Primary Sources

BACKGROUND OF THE PRIMARY SOURCE

Primary Source:_____

_____

Creator:_____

Date:_____

Background information about the source:

ANALYZING THE PRIMARY SOURCE

1. What powerful words or phrases were used?

2. What was the creator's purpose? What makes you think this was the purpose?

3. What was the primary source's audience?

Using Primary Sources

4. What biases or stereotypes did you see in the primary source?

5. What key points did the creator of the primary source make?

SUMMARIZING THE PRIMARY SOURCE

Draw two conclusions about the topic from this source. For each conclusion, provide details from the source that support it.

Conclusions	Supportive Evidence

QUESTIONS FOR FURTHER STUDY

What questions do you still have about the topic or that could guide further investigation of the topic?

Classroom Tools

Weighing Consequences

Learning and Innovation Skills	Information, Media, and Technology Skills	Life and Career Skills (Check those to be addressed)
✓ Creativity and Innovation ✓ Critical Thinking and Problem Solving ✓ Communication ○ Collaboration	○ Information Literacy ○ Media Literacy ○ Information, Communications, and Technology Literacy	☐ Flexibility and Adaptability ☐ Initiative and Self-Direction ☐ Social and Cross-Cultural Skills ☐ Productivity and Accountability ☐ Leadership and Responsibility

In this tool, students investigate a problem, weighing the consequences of various solutions, and select and defend their choice.

HOW TO USE THIS TOOL

1. For a problem to which students are seeking a solution, ask students to describe the situation, including all of the facts and circumstances that cause the problem.

2. As a class, take time to refine the problem statement so that it is truly the root of the situation.

3. Students brainstorm various solutions and note potential consequences (both positive and negative) of each.

4. Based on the potential consequences, the nature of the problem, and the situation, students select what they believe to be the best solution and give their reasons for their selection.

TIPS FOR USING THIS TOOL

• Model the activity with a situation and problem that are familiar to students and have relevance to their lives.

• Consider having students work in groups to complete the activity and share the results of their work with the whole class.

• If a situation has multiple problems, different groups of students can be assigned different problems to process. The class as a whole can identify the facts of the situation before working on potential solutions and consequences.

• Remind students to be respectful of one another's opinions and ideas.

USING TECHNOLOGY

• Post a situation and problem statement on a blog site and invite class members to contribute potential solutions and consequences.

THINKING IT THROUGH

You can address these questions during class discussion, in small groups, in student journals, or in a variety of other ways.

• What criteria did you use in evaluating the potential solutions? Do you think others would pick the same criteria? Why or why not?

• When you look for solutions to problems in your life, how might you use this process?

• How can you be sure you're working on the real problem? What is important in defining a problem?

Classroom Tools

Weighing Consequences

1. List the facts and details about the situation.

2. Define the problem that has arisen from the situation.

3. Solve it! Think of at least three solutions to the problem and summarize them below. Below each proposed solution, list the potential consequences (both positive and negative). Then circle the solution you think is best and be ready to support it.

Solution 1	Solution 2	Solution 3

Potential Consequences	Potential Consequences	Potential Consequences

Working Together Rubric

Learning and Innovation Skills	Information, Media, and Technology Skills	Life and Career Skills (Check those to be addressed)
○ Creativity and Innovation ○ Critical Thinking and Problem Solving ✓ Communication ✓ Collaboration	○ Information Literacy ○ Media Literacy ○ Information, Communications, and Technology Literacy	☐ Flexibility and Adaptability ☐ Initiative and Self-Direction ☐ Social and Cross-Cultural Skills ☐ Productivity and Accountability ☐ Leadership and Responsibility

Students can use this tool to reflect on the collaboration skills they use in any small-group learning activity.

HOW TO USE THIS TOOL

1. Conduct a class discussion about the attributes of a team player.
2. Review the "Working Together Rubric" as a class.
3. Students identify examples of each of the attributes listed under "Collaboration Skill."
4. After completing a group activity, students circle the statement for each attribute that best describes their performance as a member of a group.
5. Ask students to write about how they can improve their collaboration skills.

TIPS FOR USING THIS TOOL

• Be sure that students understand each of the attributes in the rubric before rating their own performance.

• Students could develop charts for each attribute that list examples and nonexamples.

• Ask students why it is important to be able to work collaboratively and how this might be an important quality in an employee.

• Ask students to add any additional collaboration skills that they think might be important.

• You can encourage students to track their progress in becoming a collaborative member of a team.

USING TECHNOLOGY

• Videotape small groups working together and ask students to review the video to assess their individual collaboration skills.

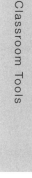

• Find video clips of other groups working together, and have students analyze the collaboration skills of the members.

• Develop an online survey of the rubric that students can use to report the assessment of their own skills. Review the compiled results of the survey and have students analyze their performance as a class. Discuss ways to improve collaboration skills as a class goal.

THINKING IT THROUGH

You can address these questions during class discussion, in small groups, in student journals, or in a variety of other ways.

• Which of the collaboration skills did you struggle with the most? What are some concrete ways you can improve your collaboration skills?

• Which of the collaboration skills caused the most problems in your team's ability to function effectively? What could you have done to improve the group's dynamic?

• Why is being able to work together effectively an important skill? How will these skills affect your future?

• Design an action plan for improving your collaboration skills. Include specific actions that you can take to become an effective team member.

Working Together Rubric

Working well in a small group or with a partner requires you to employ good listening and speaking skills, as well as good personal skills. Rate yourself on a recent collaborative activity by circling the statement for each skill that best describes you. Reflect on how you can become a better team player.

Collaboration Skill	1—Poor	2—Fair	3—Good	4—Excellent
Contributing to the Work				
Completing Assigned Tasks	Does not carry out assigned tasks.	Does assigned tasks incompletely.	Does assigned tasks, but not beyond the assignment.	Carries out assigned task in a thorough fashion.
Sharing Information	Does not share with the group.	Shares when prompted.	Volunteers to share without being asked.	Volunteers information and prompts others to do so.
Asking Appropriate Questions	Does not ask questions or asks inappropriate ones.	Asks questions that are mostly on topic.	Asks questions that relate to the topic.	Asks questions that extend the learning of the group.
Personal Skills				
Listening Attentively	Does not listen to others.	Listens some of the time; off task part of the time.	Listens actively to others and shows interest.	Listens actively to others and responds appropriately.
Getting Along	Dominates the discussion or is disagreeable.	Works together only when agreeing with the group.	Usually considerate of others' viewpoints.	Team player; tries to get the group to come to consensus.
Showing Sensitivity	Is not sensitive to the opinions or feelings of others.	Occasionally reacts to others in an insensitive manner.	Careful of the feelings of group members.	Works to engage all in the work in a positive way.

Classroom Tools

 197

Working Together Rubric

Collaboration Skill	1—Poor	2—Fair	3—Good	4—Excellent
Speaking Skills				
Presenting Ideas	Mumbles or is silent.	Thoughts are not expressed in an organized way.	Ideas are well-organized but not delivered in a clear way.	Speaks clearly and shares ideas that are well-organized.
Taking Turns	Dominates the discussion or speaks out of order.	Speaks when prompted but is sometimes out of order.	Takes turns in speaking as appropriate.	Takes turns as appropriate and prompts others to speak.

Creating Your Own 21st Century Tools

Many of the activities you already use in the classroom can enable students to develop the kind of thinking and processing of content-area concepts that they'll need to succeed in the 21st century—if you deliver them with the characteristics of the 21st century skills in mind.

You can shape existing classroom activities to promote 21st century skills by

- Reflecting on how to help students develop the four Cs of 21st century learning.
- Integrating technology.
- Helping students understand the thinking and processing skills inherent in the use of the tool.

To help you create your own 21st century tools, review the explanation of each of the components on the following page and then use the blank template to build or refine tools of your own.

Name of Tool: _____

Learning and Innovation Skills	Information, Media, and Technology Skills	Life and Career Skills (Check those to be addressed)
○ Creativity and Innovation ○ Critical Thinking and Problem Solving ○ Communication ○ Collaboration	○ Information Literacy ○ Media Literacy ○ Information, Communications, and Technology Literacy	☐ Flexibility and Adaptability ☐ Initiative and Self-Direction ☐ Social and Cross-Cultural Skills ☐ Productivity and Accountability ☐ Leadership and Responsibility

HOW TO USE THIS TOOL

Identify the steps that you and students should take for students to successfully use the tool. Be fairly explicit in defining the steps.

Identify the skills that students will be using or practicing in the tool. What you check might depend on how you plan on implementing the tool; for example, whether you use technology as a part of the activity or if you have students work in groups.

TIPS FOR USING THIS TOOL

Think about how you might use the same tool in different ways. Also note reminders for introducing or helping students learn how to use the new graphic organizer or tool.

USING TECHNOLOGY

Identify ways that you can incorporate the effective use of technology. The technology should enhance learning for students and provide them with alternative methods for completing the activity.

THINKING IT THROUGH

Draft a set of questions that can help students reflect on their own thinking and examine the cognitive processes they used in the tool. The questions can be the foundation for reflective activities, such as learning logs or journals, or can be the basis for class discussions. These questions should help students be mindful of their own learning processes.

Name of Tool: _____

Learning and Innovation Skills	Information, Media, and Technology Skills	Life and Career Skills (Check those to be addressed)
○ Creativity and Innovation ○ Critical Thinking and Problem Solving ○ Communication ○ Collaboration	○ Information Literacy ○ Media Literacy ○ Information, Communications, and Technology Literacy	☐ Flexibility and Adaptability ☐ Initiative and Self-Direction ☐ Social and Cross-Cultural Skills ☐ Productivity and Accountability ☐ Leadership and Responsibility

HOW TO USE THIS TOOL

TIPS FOR USING THIS TOOL

USING TECHNOLOGY

THINKING IT THROUGH

About the Author

Sue Z. Beers is the executive director of the Mid-Iowa School Improvement Consortium, a collaboration of approximately 160 school districts in Iowa working together to develop tools and resources for improving teaching and learning. Beers is also a member of the ASCD Faculty, working nationally and internationally with schools in the areas of literacy across the curriculum, 21st century skills, professional development planning, instructional coaching, curriculum planning, differentiated instruction, and assessment.

In addition to her current roles, Beers has been a middle and high school teacher, technology coordinator, curriculum director, and project coordinator for a statewide group of regional education agencies. She has also been a contributing writer and editor for major educational publishing companies.

As the author of six ASCD action tools and in her workshops, Beers focuses on bringing complex ideas and instructional strategies to the classroom. Her passion for ensuring that all students are successful in their learning and for preparing them to be ready for college and careers is at the heart of her work.

Beers can be reached at suebeers@netins.net.

RELATED ASCD RESOURCES: 21ST CENTURY SKILLS

At the time of publication, the following ASCD resources were available (ASCD stock numbers appear in parentheses). For up-to-date information about ASCD resources, go to www.ascd.org.

ASCD EDge® Group

Exchange ideas and connect with other educators interested in 21st century skills on the ASCD EDge® social networking site. Visit http://groups.ascd.org/groups/search and look for "21st Century Learning."

PD QuickKit®

The 21st Century Instructional Leader by Bobb Darnell (#710105S25)

Print Products

Focus: Elevating the Essentials to Radically Improve Student Learning by Mike Schmoker (#110016)

Transformational Teaching in the Information Age: Making Why and How We Teach Relevant to Students by Thomas R. Rosebrough and Ralph G. Leverett (#110078). Also available as PDF e-book.

Curriculum 21: Essential Education for a Changing World by Heidi Hayes Jacobs (#109008). Also available as PDF e-book.

21st Century Skills: Learning for Life in Our Times by Bernie Trilling and Charles Fadel (#310090)

Catching Up or Leading the Way: American Education in the Age of Globalization by Yong Zhao (#109076). Also available as PDF e-book.

Habits of Mind Across the Curriculum: Practical and Creative Strategies for Teachers by Bena O. Kallick and Arthur L. Costa (#108014). Also available as PDF e-book.

Building Literacy in Social Studies: Strategies for Improving Comprehension and Critical Thinking by Donna Ogle, Ron M. Klemp, and William McBride (#106010). Also available as PDF e-book.

The Best Schools: How Human Development Research Should Inform Educational Practice by Thomas Armstrong (#106044). Also available as PDF e-book.

Developing More Curious Minds by John F. Barell (#101246). Also available as PDF e-book.

Building Learning Communities with Character: How to Integrate Academic, Social, and Emotional Learning by Maurice J. Elias, Bernard Novick, and Jeffrey S. Kress (#101240). Also available as PDF e-book.

Professional Interest Communities

Visit the ASCD website (www.ascd.org) and click on "Prof. Interest Communities" under the "Community" tab in the left-hand navigation for information about professional educators who have formed groups around topics like "Global Education," "Interdisciplinary Curriculum and Instruction," and "Restructuring Schools." Look in the Professional Interest Communities Directory for current facilitators' e-mail addresses.

Video

Assessment for 21st Century Learning (DVD Set; #610010)

21st Century Skills: Promoting Creativity and Innovation in the Classroom (#609096)

Learning to Think. . . Thinking to Learn: The Pathway to Achievement (#607087)

For more information: send e-mail to member@ascd.org; call 1-800-933-2723 or 1-703-578-9600, press 1; send a fax to 1-703-575-5400; or write to Information Services, ASCD, 1703 N. Beauregard St., Alexandria, VA 22311-1714 USA.